THE SOVEREIGN SUN

ODYSSEUS ELYTIS, 1978

Odysseus Elytis

The Sovereign Sun

SELECTED POEMS

Translated by
KIMON FRIAR

BLOODAXE BOOKS

Copyright © Odysseus Elytis 1974, 1990
Translations copyright © Kimon Friar 1974, 1990

ISBN: 978 1 85224 120 9

This edition published 1990 by
Bloodaxe Books Ltd,
Eastburn,
South Park,
Hexham,
Northumberland NE46 1BS.

Original edition first published 1974 by
Temple University Press, Philadelphia, USA.

www.bloodaxebooks.com
For further information about Bloodaxe titles
please visit our website and join our mailing list
or write to the above address for a catalogue.

Supported by
**ARTS COUNCIL
ENGLAND**

Digital reprint of the 1990 Bloodaxe Books edition.

CONTENTS

CONTENTS

vi

CONTENTS

THE SOVEREIGN SUN

INTRODUCTION

I. Orientations

On his father's and mother's sides both, Odysseus Alepoudhélis is descended from the Aegean island of Lesbos. His father, the son of a wealthy landowner, longing to create a career of his own, left the island in early youth and went to Crete, where he founded a very successful soap factory. Returning briefly to Lesbos in order to marry, he brought his wife to Crete, and there Odysseus, the youngest of six children, was born on November 2, 1911, in the old city of Iráklion near the Minoan ruins of Knossós. Although his family left Crete in 1914, on the eve of the First World War, to settle permanently in Athens (where between 1917 and 1928 he attended the Markís School and the Third Gymnasium), the young man felt deeply proud of his Cretan birth and his Lesbian heritage. If we were to connect these three centers with a continuous line—Lesbos, Iráklion, and Athens—a broad-based triangle enclosing most of the Aegean area and its luminous islands would be formed; there the young Odysseus was to spend his summers, and its natural beauty was later to give him the images and the ethos of his poetry.

Early in his writing career, to disassociate himself from industrial connotations and to create a surname that would represent his temperament and ideals, he invented the pseudonym "Elýtis." He chose the prefix from such touchstones as *Ellás* ("Hellas"), *elpídha* ("hope"), *eleftheria* ("freedom"), and in particular from that most beautiful of all women, *Eléni* ("Helen"). Avoiding a suffix which might limit him to any particular section of Greece—such as the Lesbian *-élis*, the Cretan *-ákis*, or the Peloponnesian *-ópoulos*—he chose the general suffix *-tis*, as in the name *Polítis*, meaning "citizen." His godfather had given the child the most famous of Homeric patronymics, Odysseus, and the young poet ceaselessly re-created

3

his character to conform to this link with his ancient heritage and to the component parts of the surname he had created for himself. To name is to create.

Like most Greek children, Elýtis had dreamt of becoming an athlete until a glandular illness forced him to turn more and more to himself, to literature, magazines, novels. But as he read, he became aware that description and narrative, the logical sequence of events and speech, never touched a deeper world of which he had become aware within himself, one that stirred vaguely beneath strata of phenomena and seemed to be truer than the world of outer reality. Nothing he had read, not even poetry, seemed accurately to depict that inner validity. None of the schools of poetry dominant in his youth seemed adequate to the young man—neither the neoromanticism and traditional forms of the Parnassians, nor the pure "poetry of absence" from Mallarmé to Eluard, nor the neorealism found in Aragon; not even the various forms of symbolism, which seemed too vague, at times too allegorical, to invoke deeper, more Dionysian strains. In particular, the young idealist could not accept the attitude voiced by the "poetry of the damned" (poésie maudite) from Baudelaire to Artaud and chiefly expressed in the poets who, more than any others, were influencing his generation, Kóstas Ouránis and Kóstas Kariotákis.

The suicide of Kariotákis in 1928 added the last touch of glamor to the school of decadence. Poets, the young Elýtis felt, had locked themselves in their ivory towers; had become separated from their Greek landscape, the heritage of their own country, their demotic traditions; and now roamed in alien parks filled with autumnal rain, clouded skies, and nostalgic gardens with majestic swans where they cultivated their neuroses—the derangement of the senses, the praise of evil, all the anguish and malaise indigenous to a northern but not to a Mediterranean temperament. Paralysis and disintegration had fallen like a pall over the poets who had lived after the Catastrophe of 1897, when Greece had suffered a severe defeat at the hands of the Turks in thirty days, and even more so over those who lived after the more humiliating Disaster of 1922, when the Greeks finally gave up the idea of a Greater Greece that might rival the ancient Byzantine Empire. Although he admired the genuine poetic talent of Constantine Caváfis, who at about this time was being widely read in Greece, and the new direction indicated in this kind

4

of poetry, he could not accept the world of irony, compromise, opportunism, and decadence which it expressed with such sympathy. He was later similarly to admire and reject the work of T. S. Eliot, up to the writing of *Four Quartets;* and although he saw and admired in George Seféris, as in Caváfis, the birth of a new poetry, he could not accept the world of ruin and desolation it so mercilessly delineated.

It was surrealism which gave the young poet the key to a forbidden world whose existence he had dimly suspected but had not dared confess to himself. In 1929, at the age of eighteen, he chanced upon a book by Paul Eluard. These poems liberated the young man's imagination, gave him the direction he had gropingly sought, became the theoretical basis of his subsequent poetical quest, and impelled him to make his first tentative and shy experiments in poetry, especially during the period 1930–35 while he was attending the School of Law at the University of Athens. The year 1935, when he left the university without troubling to take his degree, was a significant year for Elýtis and for Greek letters in general. In that year he heard a lecture on surrealism by Andréas Embirícos, who had lived in Paris during the period 1925–31 and had taken part in the literary life of that capital, had associated closely with André Breton, and had been analyzed by René Laforgue. Elýtis formed a friendship that was to be lifelong with Embirícos, who became his theoretical mentor and who, in 1935, published *Blast Furnace,* the first book of surrealist automatic writing in Greece. Also in that year the young university student was discovered by another poet, George Sarandáris, who had migrated to Greece from Italy and, aware of European trends and models and burning with philosophical theories of existentialism, was writing a kind of metaphysical free verse much before his time. With great enthusiasm he introduced Elýtis to a group clustered around the new periodical, *Néa Ghrámmata (New Letters)* founded that same year by Andréas Karandónis. This magazine became the rallying center of the new poetry and prose and was the first to publish and encourage George Seféris, Níkos Engonópoulos, Níkos Gátsos, Dhimítrios Antoníou—all those who were experimenting with free verse, surrealism, and modes which were to shape the new intellectual climate in Greece. In the eleventh issue of that periodical Elýtis published for the first time his *First Poems* (1935). This was followed by groups of poems that appeared mostly

5

in *New Letters,* but also in the periodical *Macedonian Days,* in which he published "Orientations" (1936), "Hourglasses of the Unknown" (1937), and "In the Service of Summer" (1939). Some of these were circulated in reprints, then collected, with new poems, under the general title *Orientations* and presented in book form in December 1939.

Embirícos' *Blast Furnace* had been read with astonishment and ridicule. The first two books by the most uncompromising of surrealist poets, Níkos Engonópoulos, *Do Not Speak to the Conductor* (1938) and *The Pianos of Silence* (1939), were greeted with laughter and attacked gleefully for likening a girl's hair, for instance, to cardboard, her mouth to civil war, her knees to Agamemnon, her neck to red horses, her buttocks to fish glue. Even the later appearance, in 1943, of Níkos Gátsos' *Amorghós* was treated as a kind of joke, the prank of a charlatan. But Elýtis' poems, almost from the start, and with few exceptions, were hailed and praised as indicating one of the directions the new poetry might take. This was due in large part to the quality of his images and comparisons and to his lyrical adaptation of the surrealist method. Only in a few poems was Elýtis to use an automatic writing of more or less unrelated images and tropes. He soon rejected a purely uncontrolled onrush of associations, extravagant and far-fetched comparisons; for equally strong in him, though still latent, was a sense of composition which he admired, even then, in the neoclassical constructions of the poems of Andréas Kálvos (1792–1869), in whose *Odes* genuine lyricism of an ardent romanticism was controlled by neoclassical forms and techniques with some of the austerity of Pindar, another poet whom he deeply admired.

Even in his first published poems Elýtis was to show a sense of form in the shapes of his stanzas, in the number and similarity of line lengths, in the use of repetition and parallelism—qualities which in later years were to find mature fruition in his poetry. What drew him most to surrealism, however, was not its negative discarding of traditional meters and patterns but its insistence in particular that feeling, intuition, and the subconscious had a logic of their own utterly distinct from that of the conscious mind, that poetry needed no longer to unfold in a development of themes encased in previously adapted forms. He felt that surrealism heralded a return to

6

magical sources which years of rationalization had calcified, a plunge into the wellsprings of fantasy and dream, a free-flowing clustering of images creating its own shapes. He even began to discard the rigid ordering imposed by syntax and punctuation, although characteristically he retained some traditional elements, such as capitalizing the first word of each new line. He remembered acts of magic the peasant servant girls had performed at his home in Crete, and it was this magical, inner world, where nothing can or should directly be revealed, where words have the validity of deeds and burst like miracles out of a sorcerer's hat, that enchanted the young poet. His adaptation of surrealism was greatly to influence the course of subsequent poetry in Greece.

II. Sun the First

But it was Elýtis' wealth of images and associations—derived in large part from the Aegean islands, in part from his many travels throughout the length and breadth of Greece; radiant with health, joy, luminosity, and the transfiguration of adolescence—that won over poets and critics alike. The publication a few years later, in 1943, of *Sun the First together with Variations on a Sunbeam* was simply an extension of *Orientations*. Here, under a Dionysian exaltation of life not heard since the outpourings of Sikelianós, or the erotic optimism of Embiríkos, Elýtis showed himself in firmer control of his technique, more translucent in his images, clearer in his expression. In *Orientations* and *Sun the First*, he became the foremost lyric poet of his generation; in him the deification of youth amid the legendary landscape and sweet reveries of the Aegean Sea received its apotheosis. He was hailed as the poet of joy and health, of the virginal glance and the celebration of whatever was lovely, carefree, and summery in burgeoning adolescence. "Hate is for me," the young poet announced, "superfluous on the roads of the sky." His first published poem, "Of the Aegean," with its repetitive arrangement of uneven line lengths, may serve not only as an example of his strong sense of composition but also as an index to the prescribed lexicon of his early verse. In this small poem of three parts (only the first appears in this anthology), we encounter rocks, horizons, caves, and wells amid azure light and the sun; islands and archipelagoes surrounded by foam, waves, sea gulls, shells, sea breezes, and winds; seas where sailors man their ships, manipulate their dream sails and their jibs, dreaming of song, love, kisses and caresses of their betrotheds, of sunburnt girls, all in a diaphanous world that is cool, carefree, and forever dawning.

In the poems of his first two books Elýtis recalls the desolate beaches in the dazzling sun, the golden cricket husks of August in a midday sleep, the stone worn by the scorpion next to its skin, the olive groves and vineyards stretching toward the sea, the desolate march of rock, the metope of the sky, the day that stretches on its stalk, the morning inaugurations of the sea, the desolate glance that blows on stones and the deathless cacti, the barefoot winds. These poems deliberately avoid depth of perspective or the imitative realism of Renaissance painting, for in the clear light of Greece the near and the far seem to coexist on one flat plane, as in Japanese prints. Elýtis was one of the first to point out that, during the various renaissances in Europe, Greece lay enslaved as part of the Ottoman Empire, unaware of the experiments in chiaroscuro and in perspective, and still clung to the flat ideography of Byzantine icons and mosaics which in their clear linear shapes and colors were not rounded out and given body by shadows and slopes but were flattened out as though in a blazing and absolute light. He was later to become, himself, one of the foremost art critics in Greece and a lyrical painter of smooth, vivid colors and of surrealist collages that bear a sibling resemblance to his poetry. Even his admiration of Western painting tended, not toward the extravagances of Salvador Dali and other extreme surrealists, but toward the flat colors and perspectives of Matisse and the Mediterranean Picasso, toward the pointillist impressionism of Seurat and the early Pissaro.

Elýtis' poems may best be likened to Byzantine mosaics, and his images and words to the bright-colored stones, glass, and pebbles which are the alphabets of these icons (the word in Greek also means "image"). Within the icons each mosaic fragment retains its brilliance, its identity, its sharp outline; yet it is united with other, equally individual shapes, not by shading or contour, but by linear design and cluster association of colors. The mosaics Elýtis used were the pebbles, seashells, conches, grains of sand, plants, flowers, crickets, birds, and clouds of the Greek landscape in an outline of horizons and rock-island formations. Perhaps because they accepted it as their familiar everyday environment, none of the ancient Greek

8

poets had ever hymned so consistently, so ecstatically the Aegean Sea or the dazzling desolation of its landscape. Of Elýtis' generation only Nícolas Cálas (under the pseudonym Nikítas Rándos), in his *Poems* (1933), had written a few stanzas in praise of the Aegean island of Santoríni, and only George Sarandáris, who had discovered the young university student, was to influence Elýtis in images of light and color and in the deification of girls, the mistresses of rocks of whom flowers are the mirrors.

In this enchanted and enchanting summer world, Elýtis turned to the creation of a happy beauty, to "summing up his green moments," and devised youths and maidens who for an entire generation in Greece have become the glorification of whatever is carefree, daring, beautiful, adored and adoring, innocent, sexually awakening in childhood and early adolescence. For almost all Greek youths, the Greek land and seascape is an ideal paradise of water, rock, azure sky, and iridescent sun until the grimness of earning a living in this barren country takes such an early toll that in their middle twenties most young men look old beyond their years. Both in its poetry and in its prose, Greece is rich in the literature of adolescence—in Ilías Venézis' *Aeolian Earth*, Kosmás Polítis' *Eroica*, George Theotokás' *Leonis*, and Pandelís Prevelákis' *The Sun of Death*, to mention but a few modern novels. Early childhood receives its apotheosis in Elýtis' poetry, in his "Child with the skinned knee / Close-cropped head, dream uncropped / Legs with crossed anchors / Arm of pine, tongue of fish / Small brother of the cloud." This child is the "gamin of the white cloud," the "sailor boy of the garden" who "clambers up on clouds / Treads the seaweeds of the sky"; he is the "beast of the wild pear tree," who carries the sun between his thighs. The natural destiny of these boys is the "grapehard girls" who are "slowly burning because of the hydrangeas," who are "chiseled by the wind's experience," who turn into bitter-orange trees. There is Myrtó by whom Elýtis' young men are first initiated into the quivering tremors of sexual love; there is Marína of the Rocks, the "Heroine of Iambic," with a taste of storm on her lips, wandering all day long in the hard reverie of stone and sea, keeping trace in the unclothed water of its luminous days—the epitome of all that is untouchable and desired. But the unattainable ideal of all Greeks in their poetry, from ancient into modern times, has always been Helen—beauty eternally fought for and endured—whose eye-

9

lids have closed on the Hellenic landscape, who has left her ineffaceable imprint on rock and sea; an invisible music, the destination of all words, all images.

Elýtis created a "countryside of the open heart" where the innocent sky turns to serenity, where every moment is a sail that changes color, where the footsteps of time resound in the deep, and he inhabited this dream landscape with metamorphosed boys and girls, mythical maidens with floating hair and translucent bodies, "seablue to the bone," who bring in their hands an innocence as though from another world, making the invisible visible, reshaping objects according to the heart's desire, exposing the secret mystery of common things in an innocence of fused sensations where the ideal cannot be separated from the material. These lads and lasses live in a coherence of souls amid the halcyons of the afternoon where, amid innocencies and pebbles in the depths of a translucency and a "sensation of crystal," they give to the ritual of difficult dream a sure restoration. They sleep in an azure light on the stone steps of August, play with the sun at fingertips during a day carved with difficulty on the traces of the unknown where "the innocencies of anguish / Are chrysanthemum water spouts."

Elýtis created a Mediterranean land and myth in which his boys and girls can live a life, not as it is, but as they wish it to be, although nostalgically touched and corroded with taints of reality. Indeed, archaeologists recently have hazarded the theory that Atlantis, the lost Paradise, was once part of the island of Santoríni, but that in a volcanic eruption centuries ago it sank beneath the waters of the Aegean Sea, whose tidal waves inundated the Minoan city of Knossós near which Elýtis was born. The poet tried to regain this lost land of the heart's desire by creating a clear islandic consciousness, a world of sensual clarity and purity, the mysterious dawn of a new lyrical world opposed to the wasteland around him of decadence and clamor, a world synonymous with the purest forms of Hellenic character, a poetry as natural to him, as one critic has said, as though it were extensions of the pores of his body.

As in Genesis, after creating the heaven and earth, God said "Let there be light," so in Elýtis light and the sun are the Alpha and the Omega, the wellsprings of his universe. In his early poetry he created a world that breathes in an unshadowed sky, in that "radiant and productive atmosphere" in which Wallace Stevens, with whom Elýtis may best be compared, moves in Platonic clarity. Elýtis entitled his second book *Sun the First* to announce that in Greece the sun is the absolute sovereign, under whose refulgent gaze objects not only become cleared and cleansed but also dazzle away into a transillumination almost abstract—into an absolution of justice, an ethical nudity, a physical metaphysics. For Elýtis, the sun as the wellspring of light not only finds its absolute and true position in Greece but also demands continual sacrifice in order that it may be maintained, for "that the sun may revolve, great toil is required," the contribution of both the living and the dead. Although the sun and its scintillating light are one of the chief sources of imagery and metaphor in all Greek literature, in no other poet, with the exception of Níkos Kazantzákis in his *Odyssey*, have they played such a central role. What I have written of Kazantzákis' obsession with sun and light, in my Introduction to my translation of that poem, applies with equal truth to Elýtis: "The sun, flame, fire, and light compose the chief imagery of the *Odyssey*, flowing in a dazzling current throughout the poem, just as the sun in Greece itself constantly pulses throughout the clarity of its azure atmosphere, blazing on rocks, mountains, and the deviously tortured coastlines and islands of that sun-washed country . . . the sun revolves around the *Odyssey* in a protean metamorphosis."

Thus, in Elýtis, the trees drip with sun, and their branches are dipped in its oil; it enters like a triumph, swims like a river on unharvested fields, "pronounces" the young sprouts into being, glides waterdrops, hyacinths, and silence on burnt bodies, rolls its head over a meadow, lights up the poppies, plays with stones, rings its many bells, stands sentry on the topmost mast, quivers between the teeth of tomboys. Blond day is its donation, youth is its payment. Boys and girls walk under its glimmering glare, under its sieve, its semaphore; they become intoxicated with its juices, drink it like water, gulp down its vigor, learn its psalms by heart, take it for a walk, plunge into its heart, hold it between their thighs. The sun is the magical sign with which Elýtis exorcises all evil from the world, the millstone where dark and gloom are ground into a cleansing light in which Justice stands created and revealed. The Aegean, for Elýtis, is not only a geographical space, the triangle in which his

11

own personal subconscious sank its racial roots; it is also a luminous, spiritual space where the past and present of fragmented Greece promise to repossess an ethical unity.

Two poems may perhaps best exemplify Elýtis' early method and message by which he makes the intangible tangible: "The Body of Summer" and "The Mad Pomegranate Tree." Under a sky that burns so endlessly that fruit trees paint their mouths and the pores of earth open, summer is depicted as a young man sprawling naked on an Aegean beach, with crickets warming themselves in his ears, ants scurrying over his chest, lizards gliding in the long grasses of his armpits, a breath of basil on his curly groin. The pelting hail, the wintry wind, the savage billows, the thick cloud-udders are only fleeting phenomena under which the youth smiles unconcernedly, knowing truly that his deathless hour, his naked vigor will survive and persist. This personification, this plastic molding of the abstract into the concrete, is typical of Elýtis' method. The mad pomegranate tree symbolizes in his poetry all that is joyous, capricious, filled with fruit-laden laughter, source of light and sun. It unfolds its colors on high with a triumphant tremor; spreads from end to end the crocus collar of day; frolics, allures, frisks, and rages amidst the petticoats of April and the cicadas of mid-August. But just as summer survives winter in the previous poem, so the pomegranate tree in its madness skirmishes with the world's cloudy skies, shouts aloud the newborn dawning hope, shatters with light the demon's inclement weather, and pours out on the sun's bosom the giddy birds. It has become a beloved symbol in Elýtis' poetry of everything that with delirious recklessness battles whatever is evil and suffocating in the world.

Because Elýtis made the summer sensuous and tangible, deified it with a free imagination; because he turned away from the sentimentality of needless tears, so popularized by Ouránis and Kariotákis, to the substantial worth of life, to the creation of a happy beauty; and because in the midst of the world's tragedy he sang of a kindness that keeps a sword in hand, of a newborn hope that is dawning, he has been tagged and labeled as the poet only of health and joy, of hope and optimism, of radiance and youth. So ingrained has this interpretation become that it is almost impossible for admirers of his generation to consider him in any other light. It is true that this is the overall effect his early poetry strives to create, but there are, nonetheless, indications of dark clouds, inclement weather, wintry skies. Elýtis himself has never been the youths he so hymns in his poetry, except in wish fulfillment and in the transforming imagination. During his youthful years, which were spent amid family difficulties, he brooded much on suicide. He found the poetry about him fundamentally masochistic, a wasteland of spirit that conveyed man's anguish and sense of guilt; yet in his melancholy and depression the young poet found he could neither curse nor cry. Something within him impelled him to create another life in which the spirit of hope and justice would rule, to describe not what life had deprived him of but what he would like to have been given. He wanted not simply to say that life exists but in what it should consist. Joy was for him not so much a reality as a vision of paradisaical perfection which can never be achieved but must constantly be striven for.

Ultimately, Elýtis' struggle to metamorphose life, to transform it "with a boundless gaze where the world becomes / Beautiful again from the beginning according to the heart's measure" was an ethical stance: the struggle of man to create light out of darkness, to "uproot the evil crop of memory," to transmute melancholy and sorrow into joy out of an ethical need for justice, for Platonic idealization. In one of his poems he declares, "Whatever I love is born unceasingly / Whatever I love is born from the beginning." Joy for him is "the capacity of a moment that endangers the universe." *Sun the First* was published during the German-Italian occupation of Greece, and when he was asked why, in a period of such despair and darkness, he wrote poems of light and elevation, he replied that it was not the events of the age that interested him as poetry but the emotions with which these events were confronted and transfigured. Hope wells out of Elýtis from founts of melancholy and sadness, and here he differs radically from Kazantzákis, on whose tombstone in Iráklion, the birthplace of both poets, is written, "I do not hope for anything, I do not fear anything, I am free," and who in his *Odyssey* castigates "rotten-thighed Hope." The question for Elýtis is not from where one starts but where one wants to reach. A poet does not escape, he returns; he does not create solitude, he abolishes it. Poetry is the return, the infusion of spirit into the material world. The poet does not necessarily express his times; he may heroically oppose them. Out of the Aegean, Elýtis hoped to create something like a new ethical Ten Commandments, to return with a weapon of

13

light to regions where darkness reigns and makes things ugly. His need to speak of clarity and cleanliness resembles an aesthetic, an ethics, since from childhood he has identified injustice with ugliness. He knows that the sensuous objects of his poetry, his boys and girls, his summer beaches and searing sun have all, in their extensions from the outer reality in which we live, become laws which dictate, suggest, inspire, and instigate ethical acts with analogous meanings. During the early period of his life, these concepts were intuitively apprehended but were to be given comprehension and purpose in his later life and poetry.

Nor would it be correct to speak of Elýtis as the poet of optimism, as opposed to a Kariotákian pessimism. Words such as these have no meaning for him and are, indeed, simplifications of an attitude that is, at heart, ethical. This stance is what saves him from his chief danger, that of falling into sentimentality, a falsification of emotion. But for Elýtis, hatred is also a falsification, "a sentimentality of needless tears." In an interview he once declared, "My resistance to the general slogan 'we must present the drama and agony of our times' is a deep one. When reality surpasses the imagination in boldness, then poetic exaggeration becomes useless, and the affectation of pain becomes a mere coarsening of blood and tears. On the contrary, I think a poet must find those spiritual powers which may counterbalance this drama and this agony. He must aim at such a resynthesis of the fragments of reality that he may pass from 'what is' to 'what may be'." In this sense Elýtis is the direct descendant of the poets and sculptors of the classical period in Greece who idealized reality in an attempt to invoke or embody a deeper, inner reality, yet who did so by an involvement in and not a withdrawal from life and its outer necessities. A remark by Professor K. T. Denver of Saint Andrew's about classical Greek writers applies precisely to Elýtis also: "The Greek writer, like the sculptor, was more interested in creating what ought to exist instead of portraying what does; but his idea of what ought to exist was always based on an acceptance of human life as he found it."

Out of his tragedy and melancholy, out of his despair and nihilism, the poet struggled to re-create the world in his heart's image, to create concepts of beauty linked with freedom and justice, a position very similar to that Kazantzákis has taken in *The Saviors of God: Spiritual Exercises*. What is important is the stance one takes,

14

the attitude one adopts, the struggle in which one engages. All other labels are superficial and meaningless. In "With What Stones What Blood What Iron," Elýtis castigates those "who have never felt with what / Iron what stones what blood what fire / We build and dream and sing." A sympathetic reading of his early poetry will reveal, amid the blaze of summer sun and joy, some of the melancholy and nostalgia, some of the sadness and despair that well up from deep within the poet, almost without his acquiescence. His Aegean weather has its doldrums, its taints of despondency. One of his poems is entitled "Melancholy of the Aegean." In "Proud Night" he wants to write "with the fire of certainty how all that is transient on earth is nothing more than the moment we have chosen, this moment which we wish to exist beyond and above all golden contrarieties, beyond and above the disaster of death's frost." And in "Depth" he remembers "the innocence we had found so enigmatic, washed by a dawn we loved because we did not know that within us, even deeper still, we were preparing other, larger dreams that must hug in their arms more earth, more blood, more water, more fire, more love."

III. THE LOST SECOND LIEUTENANT

The dreams that in their arms were hugging so much peril exploded into crude reality when Mussolini invaded Greece from the Albanian border on the very day on which he issued his ultimatum: October 28, 1940. John Metaxás, then at the head of a dictatorial government, responded with a brief and resounding "No!" which has taken its place in Greek history with the "Come and get it" of Leonidas at Thermopylae to the Persians. As a reserve officer, Elýtis was called up immediately and, in a small room at army headquarters, was informed that he was to serve with the rank of second lieutenant in the First Army Corps. An army major and he were the first to unseal the secret order of general mobilization. The Greek people responded with delirious patriotic fever, heedless of the fact that they were setting out to meet overwhelming odds. Greece had long been aware of such an eventuality and was prepared. Within a few days, Greek troops had crossed the frontier into Albania, had driven back the Italians, and had occupied the principal towns in the South, Kóritsa and Aryirókastron. But after these initial successes, the Greeks were halted in a stalemate by the enemy's superior manpower and implements of war, and their final defeat was inevitable when the Germans invaded Greece through Yugoslavia, entering Flórina in April 1941. In May, Crete was captured in twelve days by an airborne invasion, after which all of Greece was immediately occupied by German, Bulgarian, and Italian forces, from April 1941 until September 1944, three and a half years of an occupation that was deeply to affect all subsequent Greek life and literature. The young lieutenant was impressed with what exactitude everything had been foreseen, how systematically, within a few hours, the nation had been mobilized into action. This cold-blooded mechanization vexed his inner world and made him feel it would kill poetry within him once and for all. In a letter he wrote me, Elýtis described his experience during this Albanian campaign, its consequence for his life and poetry:

> It seemed to me scandalous that, confronted by such sudden suffering and the dark and unknown future both of my country and of my personal fate, I should at all be disposed to think in poetic terms. But the sudden contrary turn given my habitual life began slowly to take on before my eyes the symbolic significance of those contraries which a poet undertakes, when he functions truly, in order to reach the one identical desired goal. Through the way up and down of Herakleitos, it became necessary for me to proceed toward that spear-point where life and death, light and darkness ceased to be contraries. Surrealism, from which I had once begun, had proclaimed the same thing to me through the mouth of André Breton. The mystical Greek tradition had again brought it to my ear through the mouth of Ángelos Sikelianós. Fear, the physical fear of war, the material fear of bombs and shells, annihilated within me all aspects of false literature and left naked the meaning of a true need for poetry. Fear was in turn annihilated in me by the salvation brought me, as a man, by a poetry made of nakedness and truth. . . .
> A kind of "metaphysical modesty" dominated me. The virtues I found embodied and living in my comrades formed in synthesis a brave young man of heroic stature, one whom I saw in every period of our history. They had killed him a thousand times, and a thousand times he had sprung up again, breathing and alive. His was no doubt the measure

and worth of our civilization, compounded of his love not of death but of life. It was with his love of Freedom that he re-created life out of the stuff of death.

Later, with an order in my pocket, I set out to meet my new army unit at the front somewhere between the Akrokerávnia Mountains and Tepeléni. One by one I abandoned the implements of my material existence. My beard became more and more unkempt. The lice swarmed and multiplied. Mud and rain disfigured my uniform. Snow covered everything in sight. And when the time came for me to take the final leap, to understand what role I was to play in terms of the enemy, I was no longer anything but a creature of slight substance who—exactly because of this—carried within him all the values of material life stressed to their breaking point and conducted to their spiritual analogy. Was this a kind of "contemporary idealism?" That very night it was necessary for me to proceed on a narrow path where I met repeatedly with stretcher-bearers who with great difficulty tried to keep in balance the heavily wounded whom they were bearing to the rear. I shall never forget the groans of those wounded. They made me, in the general over-exctitement of my mind, conjure up that "it is not possible," that "it cannot otherwise be done," which is the reversion of justice on this earth of ours. They made me swear an oath in the name of the Resurrection of that brave Hellenic Hero, who became now for me the Second Lieutenant of the Albanian Campaign, that I would advance into battle with this talisman of my lyrical idea. . . . Nothing further remained for me but to fulfill my vow, to give form to the Second Lieutenant of the Albanian Campaign on multiple levels woven together with the traditions of Greek history, but also involved—in particular—within and beyond death, in the Resurrection, the Easter of God."

But before he could fulfill his vow, the young second lieutenant wrote, between 1940 and 1943, the poems in *Sun the First*, embodiments of all Aegean beauty and adolescent dream, as though he were now describing a paradise in danger of being irrevocably lost. For this reason, perhaps, his descriptions of summer became personified and intense, his adolescents reverted to a more innocent childhood, while a melancholy, a moody heartsickness, at times ruffled the surface of a stubborn idealization. It is as though his mosaics of colored glass and pebbles had been battered here and there, not only by the devastations of time and the corroding of weather, not only by the weapons of nature, but also by man-made shrapnel and bombardment. Yet gradually the Lieutenant, returning to the marble threshing floor on which many of his comrades had fallen, began to realize that "death is that portion of life which man leaves unused." Elýtis now understood that he had at first written to give foundation to a personality endangered, later to satisfy measureless ambition, and later still to give shape to a world almost completely his own creation. He saw that most people confronted death by raising the protective barriers of subservience to duty, family, country, religion, revolution, or abandonment to hedonistic pleasure. But he saw clearly now that he could oppose death only with his poems or, as he was later to write in *Áxion Estí*, "Each with his own weapons, I said: / At the Pass I'll deploy my pomegranates / at the Pass I'll post my zephyrs guard." He felt a deep need now to write a poetry of nakedness and truth. Casting aside an easy patriotism, he nevertheless became aware within himself of a proud nation's consciousness. Conscience and consciousness became for him the only possible substitutes for religion in a dedication to an Unknown God, though he readily embraced the symbols and rituals bequeathed him by his Byzantine tradition. He saw in the heroic resistance of the Greek people against superior odds, throughout their long history, a recklessness of spirit, a divine madness. In the spontaneous reaction of the Greek people to Mussolini's invasion, he saw the victory of a beautiful rashness over self-calculation, an instinct that could distinguish between good and evil in a time of danger.

In an agonized need to speak of the dreadful events in which he had participated not in imagination only but also in a reality of lice and gunpowder, Elýtis now turned to a poetry less surrealist and more naked. The complexity and turmoil of his emotions made it evident to him that he needed the scaffolding of a long poem, and in 1943 he wrote his *Heroic and Elegiac Song for the Lost Second Lieutenant of the Albanian Campaign*. This poem, however, does not have an orderly structure but is, rather, a symphonic arrangement of themes and counterthemes loosely strung together, a "spearpoint where life and death, light and darkness" cease to be contraries and become interwoven and involved one with the other. His verse line now departs from the irregularity of free verse and hovers around the traditional fifteen-syllable line of demotic poetry, which is similar in effect to our traditional blank-verse line. His images still retain the daring and strangeness, the free associations of far-flung comparisons given him by surrealism and which he was never to abandon, but these are now deliberately subdued to the service of greater clarity, to the fulfillment of a vow, to a need to find national identification and thus speak not only for himself but also for his nation.

The Second Lieutenant of *Heroic and Elegiac Song* is, of course, the same boy with the skinned knee, the same gamin of the white cloud of his earlier poetry, who has now come of age. He had been the small sailor of the garden whose music hall of flowers had suddenly been abandoned by the birds. He had been the same sturdy lad who, like Robert Frost's boy climbing birches, had once "defied the peach tree leaves," or could have been found "scratching the sun on a saddle of two small branches." He had roamed with a twig of pomegranate in his teeth, kissing in reverence the desolate island pebbles. He had been the first to join in the folk dances of the angels, or, in the arms of the bitter-orange girls at night, to have soiled "the large garment of the stars." But now he is called upon, like so many heroes of Greek demotic songs, to wrestle with Charon on "the marble threshing floor." Now "agony stoops with bony hands" and "smothers the flowers upon her one by one." Whereas in "Body of Summer" the youthful personification had smiled indolently under the pelting hail and the claws of the wintry wind, serenely knowing he would again find his deathless hour and his naked vigor, now "winter enters up to the brain." Evil flares up, vultures share the bread crumbs of the sky, clouds become howling wolves, and God himself smells of mulehide and gunpowder. The young Lieutenant lies on his scorched battle-coat, a bullet hole between his eyebrows, "a small bitter well, fingerprint of fate." At his side—as though amputation were not so much an irreplaceable severance of what had been as the promise of growth to come—lies his "half-finished arm." His body is a silent shipwreck of dawn, his mouth is a small songless bird, his hands are prairies of desolation.

But "death is that portion of life which man leaves unused," and Elýtis' orientation, particularly in the face of annihilation, has always been one of affirmation in humanity, in racial conscience and consciousness, in justice, in liberty, in the resurrection and transfiguration implied by the very act of writing, of composing, of dreaming, so that the poet may "torment secret evil wherever it may be." Thus turning, as he was more and more to do, to symbols in the ritual of the Greek Orthodox Church to give him weapons, Elýtis has the Lieutenant ascend "alone and blazing with light," so drunk with light that his heart shines through, while "Around him those passions glow that once were lost in the solitude of sin." Easter bells peal out in the soldier's transfiguration and proclaim "Tomorrow, tomorrow, tomorrow: the Easter of God." "I believe," Elýtis once wrote me, "in the restitution of justice, which I identify with light. And together with a glorious and ancient ancestor of mine, I am proud to say, in spite of the fashion of my time, that 'I do not care for those gods whose worship is practiced in the dark.' "

IV. TRANSITIONS

At this time Elýtis also turned for identification to another poet who in another war had been propped up against a wall and shot by fascists, to Federico García Lorca, and in 1948 translated some of his poems. The boy with the skinned knee had symbolically died in the snows of Albania, had been embalmed and buried in Elýtis' heart, had been put away, but had stubbornly refused to be forgotten. Elýtis was himself no longer the young men he had deified, but neither could he completely accept the man of duty and conscience he was becoming. The following ten years were anguished ones for him, during which he traveled much, participated in many outer activities out of a sense of responsibility and national duty. As an art and literary critic, he attempted to formulate an aesthetic and mold a way of life that would be more relevant to the world about him, yet would not lose those essential virtues which were the foundations of his character and poetic validity. He said farewell to the enchanting dreams of his youth in a long and lingering departure, for although during the years 1947–56 he wrote many poems and essays on aesthetic matters, he destroyed almost all of them, seeing that neither his poetry nor his theories had progressed much beyond his earlier work. Nevertheless, stubbornly resisting powers of annihilation, he struggled to formulate new standards of belief and art, thus solidly building the foundation of his mature work.

In 1948 a number of periodicals in Italy, England, and the United States began to publish translations of his poetry. He was appointed regular critic of the Athens newspaper *Kathimeriní (Daily)*, but needing a change of place as well as a change of heart, he settled in Paris that same year, studying literature at the Sorbonne. With Paris as a base he traveled throughout England, Switzerland, Italy, and Spain until 1952. In Europe he associated closely, not only with the poets Breton, Eluard, Tzara, Char, Jouve, Michaux, and Ungaretti, but also with the painters and sculptors compatible to his nature and about whom he wrote many articles: Matisse, Picasso, Giacometti, and de Chirico, among others. He collaborated with the periodical *Verve*, writing his articles in French. In 1948 he represented Greece in the Second International Gathering of Modern Painters in Geneva and in 1950 participated in the First International Conference of Art Critics in Paris. In that same year he was elected a member of the International Union of Art Critics. On his return to Greece in 1953, he was elected a member of The Group of Twelve, a prestigious committe which every year gave awards to the best books published in poetry, essay, and drama. During 1945–46 he had served as director of programming and broadcasting for the National Broadcasting Institute in Athens and now served again in 1953–54. During 1955–56 he served on the governing board of Karolos Koun's Art Theater in Athens; during 1956–58 as president of the Governing Board of the Greek Ballet; and during 1965–68 as a member of the Administration Board of the Greek National Theater. Elýtis' participation in the Albanian Campaign; his endurance during the Occupation and the Civil War that followed; his immersion in civic, cultural, and artistic affairs; his travels; the widening of his horizons in international assemblies—all these served to fill a gap, for almost ten years, during which, suffering internal as well as external change, he found it extremely difficult to make the painful transition, to merge and unite a deeper inner reality with an insistently encroaching outer reality. Time no longer went by "like leaves like pebbles," but became a "frenzied sculptor of men." But finally, in 1959, he published *Áxion Estí*, and in 1960, *Six and One Remorses for the Sky*.

v. Remorses

Though published two years later than *Áxion Estí*, the two versions of "Sleep of the Valiant" in *Remorses* had been written in 1953, and the other poems in that book were written concomitantly with

21

those in *Áxion Estí,* that is, during the years 1956–58; like pendant jewels hung on a necklace of matched precious stones, the light of one reflected and illuminated the light of the others. All the poems in *Remorses* show the poet in his full maturity, come to terms at long length with the tragic element in the world. These poems are, nevertheless, remorses, regrets, pangs of conscience and guilt for the lost azure sky, for the *ouranós* (the word in Greek means both "sky" and "heaven"), for a sky no longer innocent or pellucid, or "deep and unchanging," as he had once written, but overcast and cloudy, polluted, bombarded and torn until "nothing but the shattered echo" remained. It had now become an embattled region where not just a single soldier or armies of men but all mankind struggled in the field of the universe with eternal antagonists, for the stone gods had leapt to life out of the metopes of the sky, brandishing their lightnings and thunderbolts.

One of the six poems, "Sleep of the Valiant," is written in two versions. The first thirteen lines of each poem are the same, but the first version has a coda of three, the second a coda of six lines. In both versions the boy with the skinned knee of the Aegean islands and the dead Lieutenant of the Albanian Campaign have become valiant symbols of mankind battling with the mysterious powers of the universe that are no longer oppositions of good and evil but an agonizing and mystifying correlation of both, powers that are destructive and creative at once—the *élan vital* in all of nature—as in Bergson, as in Kazantzákis. Like Milton's Satan, Elýtis is tormented by "the thought / Both of lost happiness and lasting pain," for his valiants have also been "hurled headlong flaming from the ethereal sky / With hideous ruin and combustion down / To bottomless perdition." They smell of frankincense, their features have been "scorched from their passage through the Vast Dark Places" where "the Immovable suddenly hurled them / Prone." But Elýtis' valiants do not lie in adamantine chains and penal fire, for in those Tartarean depths they have finally been released by Time, and their ancient immemorial blood reverts once more into the bloodstream of the universe where, laboriously, it begins to be metamorphosed again into a new Sun dispelling "the oracle-making powers of Darkness." Worlds begin to be re-created from a beginning in which glows "a creation of avenged emotions," and through which the Valiants pass, "the Executioner slain within them," but now no longer as innocent lads under a clear Aegean sky, but as "Peasants of the infinite azure," cultivators of limitless meadows. This is where the main movements of both versions end.

In the coda of the first version, the Valiants are depicted in their tragic courage. Vultures swoop down to savor their clay entrails and their blood, but their footfalls are now annulled; unlike the Aegean lad "Drinking the Corinthian sun / Reading the marbles," they now "read the world insatiably with eyes forever open." In the coda of the second version, the Valiants wander in an ageless Time, restoring "to things their true names," in a "rage of innocence." Into a world that was rotting out of ignorance (for evil, according to Plato, is the consequence not so much of malignancy as of ignorance), and where men "inexplicably had committed their dark iniquities," Arete descends. Elýtis identifies her with both the Virgin Mary and Greece itself, a girl who performs miracles and who is not the heavy personification of the Latin Virtus but a maiden with a lean, boyish body. This ancient Greek word, still used today as a girl's name, is untranslatable in English by any word, for it connotes goodness, moral virtue, kindness, valor, courage, glory, and excellence of every kind. Arete, who now descends to the Vast Dark Places and labors to turn darkness into light, is the apotheosis here of all Elýtis' Aegean girls—Mirtó, Marína, and Eléni. In these poems Elýtis has embraced the tragic element in life, the vultures, the injustice, the powers of darkness. Upholding his affirmation with stoic courage, he acknowledges evil as an element almost equal to goodness but still reads the world insatiably with eyes forever open, with nostalgia that rises as though from the "crevices in the sleep of the Valiant."

"Laconic," "Beauty and the Illiterate," and "The Other Noah," all written in 1956, the year in which he began writing *Áxion Estí*, are further extensions of evil and the poet's defiance. "Well then," he says in acceptance, "he whom I sought *I am*." In times "that have warped the rainbow," when the poet has been orphaned from light, when men gnaw at one another's entrails as in Dante's Inferno, when Evil is concentrated in "all-devastating uranium," and when God erred by letting fall over men's impious toil "drop by drop / The trills of Paradise," the poet accepts, like another Noah in the Ark of his asceticism, not the dove but the humble sparrow. He saves also a few words, *"bread, longing, love,"* and deifies the holy day of sensual pleasure when even lust itself, defined as the ecstasy of the senses, attains an elemental, pre-Christian innocence. For the modern Greek, the Platonic Ideal or Idea may only be reached by means of the senses which through purification and sanctification justify the demands even of lust. Almost without desiring it, by following the regal road of the senses and probing the metaphysics of light, Elýtis arrived at an ethical paradise freed of the falsifications of theologians. As in "Seven Days for Eternity," the poet longs to preserve the sound a flowerpot makes as it shatters in empathy with the great pleasure derived "At the very moment the gardener's daughter is being kissed secretly in the back yard." Light is now not simply the luminosity of sun and sky, the radiance in which the Lieutenant ascended in the Easter of God, but radiates from "a conflagration that consumes all my possessions," for the poet has tragically learned that the most execrable noises are heard not in the world's hurly burly or the detonations of bombs but "in utter quietude," in the unbearable loneliness in the heart of man. This is how Beauty is born, not in dream and withdrawal, but in that struggle with evil from which stars are scattered and sown. In these poems Elýtis has written a variation on Keats' enigmatic conclusion in "Ode on a Grecian Urn," as though he were saying "Beauty is justice, justice beauty,—that is all / Ye know on earth, and all ye need to know."

In "Origin of Landscape or The End of Mercy," written in 1958, the poet recalls the days when he "labored to make the endless azure so tender" and discovers that purity and innocence are not so much given qualities in youth as searing products which a man attains when he confronts himself in merciless honesty as he walks this world once more "without gods, but heavy with the burden of whatever, in living, I had snatched away from death." Purity, for Elýtis, now has nothing to do with the moralizing sense of abstention; on the contrary, it connotes the full participation in and accomplishment of desire that go beyond Christian ethical codes. And in one of the most moving poems he has written, "The Autopsy" (1957), the poet performs a dissection on himself, permitting the knife to penetrate only there where "the intention sufficed for the Evil." Evil had been confronted by the dead poet, not in a posture which had been terrified, but in one which is terrifying to the beholder in its innocence. In the depths of the poet's heart the surgeon finds the gold of the olive root, in his blood "ample traces of azure," in his left ear "a few grains of delicate, extremely fine sand," and on his groin a few "flakes of fire." When his heart was cut open, the cries of birds had burst out "which in hours of great loneliness he had learned by heart." Pricked with pangs of conscience, burdened with remorse and reconciliation, acknowledging the pollution of the azure sky and the heavens, Elýtis now asserts his lyricism with a grave and somber voice, rifted with strains of the tragic.

VI. AXION ESTI

And yet the poems of *Remorses* are but finger exercises to the great symphonic poem he was writing concomitantly, *Áxion Estí*. Few better examples than these two books can be found in literature of a poet's stubborn ability to grow, to change, to mature, to reach in some regard a position almost diametrically opposite to that from which he began, and yet to retain integrally the basic parts which from the beginning composed his personality and temperament. A comparable example is Wallace Stevens' growth in technique and metaphysics from, say, *Harmonium* to *Notes toward a Supreme Fiction*, or perhaps better still that of William Butler Yeats from the romantic mysticism of his early poetry to the transcendental realism of his late period. But whereas Yeats summed up his creative imagination and philosophy in a book of poetic prose, *A Vision* (which, had he written it in verse, would have been one of the greatest poems of all time), Elýtis embodied his speculations, his growth, his change from personality to character, in a long, extremely complicated poem in which he sums up his mature thought and feeling. I know of few long poems with formal structures so intricate. It is a tribute to Elýtis' ability for metamorphosis. We have seen that the young poet, who had begun with the free-floating associations of surrealism, and whose images were clusters of mosiacs in an obscure ideogram, had nevertheless, even from his earliest poem, sensed the need for harmony, proportion, balance, and structure which, for him, were the bones and silhouette of beauty. He had long been dreaming of a poem which would combine within itself the consequences of contemporary experiences he had undergone, particularly in the Second World War and its aftermath, but at the same time would be as well knit and as strong in structure as an ode by Kálvos or Pindar. This he achieved in *Áxion Estí*.

Áxion Estí, in Greek, is the phrase "Worthy it is," which occurs often in the Divine Liturgy of the Greek Orthodox Church, "Worthy

it is to glorify Thee, verily the Mother of God," and is the name
of a holy icon of the Virgin Mary in a monastery on Mount Athos.
It also occurs in several hymns, particularly in a long funeral hymn
sung on Good Friday which begins, "Worthy it is to glorify Thee,
the Giver of Life, Thou who didst extend Thy hand upon the Cross,
and shatter the power of the enemy. Worthy it is to magnify Thee,
the Creator of all; for by Thy sufferings we are freed from suffering
and delivered from corruption."

The poem is divided into three parts. In Part I, "Genesis," the poet
autobiographically depicts his life—but symbolically, that of all
poets—from the first day he saw light to manhood when he first
came face to face with the dangers of this world. On another plane,
together with the poet is born "this small, this great world": the
small world according to the poet's or an individual's apprehension
or to the limitations of his senses, the small world that is Greece, but
also the representative of the great world of the universe, micro-
cosm and macrocosm, not one within the other but each inter-
changeably the other, a new cosmology. Every time a child is born,
the world is born with him. Like the biblical Genesis, this part is
divided into seven sections depicting the creation of land, sea,
plants, flowers, and animals, and also the development of the Greek
language from Homer to the present day. The poet speaks twice,
first in the first-person singular and then in the third person, for he
also represents the Platonic eternal Self, who exists before birth,
who knows everything, who guides the poet toward God, talking,
advising, explaining the mysteries of the world. This is a technique
reminiscent of some Picasso figures in which one sees the same head
from different points of view simultaneously. Five of these seven
sections ends with the same refrain, "this small, this great world."
As a whole the sections show a development from dawn to sudden
dusk, from childhood to manhood, from innocence to knowledge of
an Evil often equated with war, all interwoven in a pattern parallel
to the poet's own thematic autobiography. There is no reference to
afternoon in this part, for night falls abruptly after midday, as war
fell suddenly on the poet in the middle journey of his life. Midday,
the blaze of noon, has always been for Elýtis the zenith, the climax-
ing moment in the balancing scale that is Greece and that weighs, in
equilibrium, light on the one scale and instinct on the other. All of
Part I is written in free verse, not in the free-flowing rhythms of a
Whitman, but in cadences of shorter length where the poet is highly

conscious of the technical and rhythmical relations of one line to another in terms of movement and enjambment, as though he were walking on an unknown surface where he must make certain of his footing at every step.

Part II, "The Passions," is composed of three categories—Psalms, Odes, and Reading—which are mathematically grouped in three sections. Each of the three sections is arranged thus: two Psalms, an Ode, a Reading, an Ode, two Psalms, an Ode, a Reading, an Ode, two Psalms; that is, PPOROPPOROPP. Each section, in other words, contains six Psalms, four Odes, and two Readings. The entire Part II, therefore, contains eighteen Psalms, twelve Odes, and six Readings. The first section has as its theme the development of consciousness within tradition, the second the development of consciousness within danger, and the third the development of consciousness in the overcoming of danger. The Psalms, for which Byzantine troparia and the Psalms of David are the models, are written in free verse and grouped in pairs. The Odes, one on either side of the Readings, are written in a highly elaborated version of syllabic versification familiar to American and English readers in the poetry of Marianne Moore, but with many additional complications, some of which I have described in the Notes to this volume. The Readings, which constitute the spine of this middle part, are written in an extremely simple form of demotic prose modeled on the style of General Yánnis Makriyánnis (whose *Memoirs* has become a touchstone of modern Greek prose style) and take the place of those excerpts read from the Bible in the Liturgy of the Greek Orthodox Church as Gospel Readings. The subject matter, however, is entirely contemporary and, in particular, is a realistic and graphic description, yet exalted and transcendent, of the poet's experience, now given its final form, as a second lieutenant in the Albanian Campaign. Their titles give some indication of the contents: "The March to the Front," "The Mule Drivers," "The Great Retreat," "The Plot of Land with the Nettles," "The Courtyard of Sheep," and "Prophetic." I have represented the Readings here with the last, which, although not typical of the descriptions of war and its terrors, nevertheless sums up the poet's ethical stance on these events.

Part III, the "Gloria," is a doxology, a laudation of the phenomena in Elýtis' personal mythology. All phenomena, whether good or evil, are embraced in an ecstasy of praise, their ephemeral elements glorified in the verses begun with *now*, their eternal essence in those beginning with *aye*. Like the triple doorway in a Byzantine church, where the central portal is larger than the flanking entrances, Part III is composed of three sections of similar structure, of which the middle is the longest. The first and third sections are ordered in the following manner: six quatrains, a triplet, six quatrains, a triplet, five quatrains, seven couplets. Further complications of meter, rhyme, and technique are described in the Notes.

I know of no other poem either in English or in Greek which has a comparable complexity of structure. Eliot's *Four Quartets* has a complicated thematic counterpointing, a musical elaboration of ideas, but the architectural structure, in comparison with that of *Áxion Estí*, is relatively simple. Elýtis found it impossible to attempt a work of great length and spirit—one that would sum up his experience, his growth, his maturity, his personal mythology, his awakened consciousness, his national identification—without the foundation of an initial plan that would give him the assurance and the grandeur an epical-lyrical work involves. He felt the need to return, not to the rejuvenation of old forms, but to the creation of new ones, new limitations which the poet himself would arbitrarily establish so that the struggle with structure, pattern, order, meter, stanza, and orchestration would create a tension, throw out sparks, deepen thought, and achieve a new freedom in which the flight of the imagination and a free-flowing association of images are not caged but, on the contrary, are given wings and strength to reach greater heights. A comparable tension between content and composition, on a smaller scale, may be found in the poems of Gerard Manley Hopkins and Dylan Thomas. Ultimately in such a poem, Elýtis' intention has been to formulate an aesthetic, an ethic, a metaphysics. His elaborate techniques and stanzaic shapes are not only patterns of words and lines arranged on a page but are also Time itself better apprehended by being cut and portioned out in comprehensive intervals. All long poems such as *Áxion Estí*, *The Waste Land*, or *The Cantos* have always set the tone and imagery for shorter poems written after their advent. As Elýtis himself has demonstrated by writing the *Remorses*, or Yeats by writing the poems which depend on *A Vision*, *Áxion Estí* is bound, in the years to come, to convince younger poets that it is now possible for contemporary experience to pass from its romantic into its classic phase with no loss of intensity.

Áxion Estí is also a rich treasure of the Greek tongue, for Elýtis is aware that he has been "given the Hellenic tongue," that his house is "a humble one on the sandy shores of Homer." He has kept to a strict demotic base with taste and discretion, but he has also added to his lexicon, grammar, syntax, and rhythm embellishments taken from all periods of Greek literature—from the Septuagint, the Byzantine troparia, the demotic songs and folk legends of the medieval period; from *Erotókritos*, Makriyánnis, Solomós, Kálvos, Sikelianós, Palamás, Papadhiamándis—and he has coined words of his own. Throughout his entire career he has been primarily interested in the plastic use of language, manipulating words and images like a painter or sculptor, shaping and reworking them as though they were colors or material. He has shaken off the tyranny of the speech of the common man, together with that of the pseudo-educated, whose *katharévousa* (an artificially constructed language based on Attic Greek) are both strangleholds on the creative spirit. He has returned to the language of the poet-saint, the prophet who must utter his vision in a common liturgy. He has shown that if a poet has taste and discrimination he can employ organically all aspects of the Greek tongue to enrich the demotic language with which imaginative writing, in all periods, has flourished. *Áxion Estí* has become a kind of New Testament of the Greeks in which the poet's consciousness has transformed the world, according to Elýtis' youthful intentions, and "made it beautiful again according to the heart's measure."

In *Áxion Estí*, Elýtis makes use of all his earlier symbols and images derived from nature. They are named one by one, lovingly caressed as never before, placed in a sacred hierarchy. "This then is I," he announces in Psalm I, "created for young girls and the islands of the Aegean / lover of the roebuck's leap / and neophyte of the olive trees / sun-drinker and locust-killer." But also, he laments in Ode 5, "my girls are in mourning, . . . my young men bear weapons." Now his images take on their deepest, their highest, their most ethical meaning, for they have become a system of symbols derived from a transfiguration of nature's elements into spiritual essence. For centuries the Greek islanders have used white-wash, a composition of lime and water, as a cleansing element with which yearly to whiten the walls of their houses until their dazzle, set against azure sky and sea, has become for all a symbol of clarity, purity, and luminosity. In a new, as yet unpublished poem, Elýtis speaks of "Light-years in the skies, virtue-years in the whitewash," as though there exists a measurement for ethical distances in white-wash comparable to astronomical distances in the heavens. In his early poems he had sung of whitewashed courtyards, of white-washed dawns, of a whitewash "that bears all noons on its back," and even of casting horizons into the whitewash to whiten the four walls of his future. Finally, in *Áxion Estí*, he abstracts whitewash into the transcendent realm of Ideas when, in the last Psalm of "The Passions," he declares, "Now in whitewash I enclose and entrust / my true Laws." Here the cleansing purity of whitewash has been transported to an ethical level of invisible Platonic *Laws*, to new Commandments by which to live, a new asceticism. Here is trans-formation from a physical to a moral condition without loss of natural beauty.

Although symbols and myths from Classical and Hellenistic times are almost obsessively used by modern Greek poets such as Caváfis, Kazantzákis, and Seféris as part of their living heritage, Elýtis has used them sparingly, preferring to create his own personal myth-ology out of his evolving experience; out of the Greek landscape and mores; out of the Greek historic consciousness in its long struggle for freedom; out of the development of the Greek language as one integral whole; out of the liturgy of Byzantine hymnology and the Orthodox Church, with its sublimations of Dionysian and Eleusinian mysteries; and primarily out of the sea, sky, rock, and whitewash of his contemporary Aegean environment. In the doxology, in an ec-stasy of reconciliation, he names one by one whatever in the world is intense or subtle, vivid or humble, contrary or paradoxical, good or evil, and in his march to a "distant and sinless land" he discovers that "it is the hand of Death / that bestows Life," and that ulti-mately, though mankind must struggle ceaselessly for freedom and justice, for the triumph of good over evil, life must, nevertheless, be accepted in its total necessity. He concludes, with sadness and reso-lution, that "WORTHY is the price paid," a phrase that sums up his poetic and ethical evolution.

VII. Villa Natacha and Constandinos Paleologhos

After the publication of *Áxion Estí*, Elýtis spent March through June of 1961 touring the United States at the invitation of the Depart-ment of State, visiting Washington, New Orleans, Sante Fe, Los Angeles, Chicago, Buffalo, and New York. But in December 1962, as though to keep the balance straight, he accepted an invitation from the Soviet Union and for a month visited Odessa, Moscow, and Leningrad. During the next few years he occupied himself in collecting and correcting his prose work in *Open Book*, primarily essays on aesthetic matters, and in working on a long poem, *María Nephéli*, a dialogue between a poet and a girl, in which for the first time his images are derived primarily, not from nature, but from urban life. After the military coup of the colonels of April 21, 1967, he was unable to write in the hampered atmosphere, and, longing to breathe a freer air, left for France, where he lived from May 1969 to July 1971, spending the summer of 1970 visiting friends in Cyprus. Living primarily in Paris, on Saint Germain-des-Prés, entertaining and being entertained by friends, he set aside once more the writing of his urban poem and, in a nostalgic re-creation typical of so many Greek poets throughout the centuries who have lived in exile, once more invoked the Aegean landscape, its sun, its sea, its light. In "Prophetic" he had asked, "Exiled Poet, tell me, what do you see in your century?" and in these subsequent poems he has borne witness not only to what he has seen but also to what he has envisaged through the true light of the imagination, for "the time has come for dreams to be avenged." This was a highly productive period, which resulted in four poems, each elegantly published as a separate book: *Villa Natacha* and *Death and Resurrection of Constandínos Paleológhos*, written in 1969; *The Monogram* and *The Sovereign Sun*, written in 1970; and a collection of poems, *The Light Tree and the Fourteenth Beauty*, written in 1971 although many had been contemplated since 1969.

Before going to Paris, Elýtis stopped for a while at the Villa Natacha of his old friend and compatriot, Tériade, the famous art connoisseur, publisher of art books, and editor of the epoch-making periodicals *Minotaure* and *Verve*. Here on Saint Jean-Cap-Ferret between Nice and Monte Carlo, in a villa implanted amid a famous garden and studded with priceless treasures of modern masters, Elýtis wrote "Villa Natacha." Unhappy over the turn of political events in Greece, smoking his first free cigarette amid plants with strange names, the poet—a bird warbling in a time of war—connects in reverie through communicating seas the Greek and French regions of the Mediterranean. He upholds the free or simple man "wearing a plain white shirt" who in a time of Evil treads on the ogres of psychology, politics, and sociology as Destiny cracks in an unrecognized moment, as one takes in proportion to what one has given.

In one of several statements that may serve as leitmotifs to his poetic faith, Elýtis here declares that "We've worshipped danger long enough, and it's time it repaid us." Just as Matisse, that genius of omission, revolutionized painting by turning away from chiaroscuro, perspective, and tone toward flat plains and simple forms, so the poet dreams of a revolution away from Evil and wars. If only he could find the right stance, then Man, "Evil without wanting to be" —with only a slight swerve of the wheel, as in an accident, but in the opposite direction—would have within his horizon the end of wars, the downfall of tyrants, the remission of sexual shame.

In *Death and Resurrection of Constandínos Paleológhos*, Elýtis pays a lingering tribute to his Byzantine heritage. The last of the Byzantine emperors, who died in 1453 defending the walls of Con-stantinople against the Turks, Paleológhos symbolizes both the fall of Byzantium and its resurrection. He has become for the Greek people one of those godlike figures whose ritual deaths are simply hibernations for more glorious awakenings. Because in this poem he is both beleaguered medieval king and contemporary poet upholding the eternal Greek tradition under attack by the younger Turks of our modern generation, the idealist fighting against odds, Elýtis at times invokes his own childhood on the island of Spétsas. Through-out many of his poems Elýtis often speaks on two levels, one uni-versal or objective, the other personal or subjective. King and poet merge into one in their attempt to maintain the Greek tradition and its poetry; to make "noon out of night—all life in a radiance"; to rise in resurrection above ruins, debris, horses, and carcasses thrown on dumpheaps, the king with a broken lance in his hand, the poet with an unbroken word between his teeth, both struggling to bring Paradise to their measure, the last of the Hellenes. The first part concludes with what was first enunciated in *Áxion Estí*, another basic leitmotif of Elýtis' entire work: "The world's an oppressive place to live through   yet with a little pride it's worth it."

VIII. THE LIGHT TREE

As Elýtis approached sixty he became more and more confirmed in the magical, the revelatory nature of poetry. The poems in *The Light Tree* bear witness again and again to those sudden messages from infinity preceded by raps and flashes and announced by a girl flying in annunciation or sexual invitation; by the passage of a bird; by the utterance of rock or tree; by a dive into the sun or sea; by a remembrance, as in Wordsworth or Vaughan, of an angel infancy when the child, and later the adolescent, still glowed with the reflection of another, unsullied land of origin. Thus in "Palm Sunday," the day of Christ's triumphant entrance into Jerusalem and the poet's into his Paradise, the reverie of a girl with unbuttoned blouse, a bird descending with a twig in its beak become carriers of an apocalypse when everything seems suspended in the air in an immobile moment of eternity. If only Nature can be "read" intuitively it may utter the ultimate mystery in sudden flashes and messages wherein all man's questions about the why and wherefore may be answered. It is, however, the very nature of such revelation that on awakening from the suspending trance one has forgotten the answer, though a deep pervading glow persists that it *had* been disclosed. Words are always the betrayers of the vision. Thus in "Three Times the Truth" the poet, feeling in his despair that "something must *assuredly* exist," seeks for truth in Nature, in birds and rockpools, for words are not enough: "When words withdraw what can one possibly say?" In the vast silence following upon catastrophe, small, almost inaudible sounds are heard. Out of rosemary, out of springs, words form into the daily prayer of our need. Straining to decode the mysterious rustlings in the wind and the trees, words "as strange and enigmatic" as those heard in "Genesis V"—Roes, Esa, Arimna, Nus, Morimlatity, Yletis—but which contain much of his destiny—Eros, Sea, Marina, Sun, Immortality, Elýtis—the poet babbles "What do you know of me?" and out of half-formed words that now presage abyss, death, and dream, he creates, out of nothing, his own cryptographic meaning, his own truth. Nevertheless, living amid these simple yet profound phenomena, the poet re-creates them and on them imposes his own meaning, his own imprint, for "out of nothing" is born our Paradise. In "What Can't Be Done," he realizes that in this place and space of ours in the universe, where in a little while it becomes dark forever, where men have come to an end and nothing of importance remains to be said, the poet can only measure himself by these salvages from the shipwreck of time and try to do what can't be done, to say what can't be said. This is his despair and his salvation.

One of Elýtis's basic images for the moment of revelation is a dive into water which is at the same time a plunge into the sun. In this image opposites become one (whether water and fire or life and death), and the way up and the way down of Herakleitos lead to the same destination. This is best seen in "Delos," in the island birthplace of Apollo, God of the Sun, whose rays in Elýtis' mythology are mightier than the thunderbolts of Zeus. Plunging into those mythological waters, entering thus a Platonic realm of white abstraction and purification, the poet passes "straight into the heart of the sun" and from this baptism emerges as fresh as a newborn babe glowing with divine light. But this regeneration, this resurrection, is granted only to those who have learned to say "I love," for in Elýtis, as in Dante, creation may be glorified only by love. Thus, also, in "The Garden with the Scorched Hand," in a moment of suicidal despair, he dives into an underwater world and garden where, although the poet is inverted, feet up and head down, all seems righted, for when he hit bottom, head on, "a sun leaped up   The ether splayed out like rays," until in ecstasy and recognition he cries out "Sun my sun my very own   Take all I have take it all   and leave me pride   That I may not reveal a single tear   That I may only touch you even though I burn." He stretches out his hand in salvation and sacrifice, but the garden—lost and found and lost again—vanishes, and the poet once more confronts mundane realities about him, the disasters of man's condition where he must "struggle with the Not and the Impossible of this world." What remains is a scorched hand to remind him that dream, too, is a reality.

The apotheosis of light, however, comes to its zenith in the title poem, "The Light Tree." If in "The Garden with the Scorched Hand" the young man contemplates suicide in a moment of despair, here he contemplates it in a moment of intense happiness, that he might not once again waken into a world of disillusionment or note what deformations man has caused in nature. He can no longer confront the world of imperfection as he recalls a lost Paradise and broods on "the wronged man" within him. As he remembers how "Once or twice the Perfect appeared before my eyes   and then nothing once more," such a moment of revelation comes and, as is most often the case, at the most unexpected, the most insignificant time: while he leans out of the window to see how far into the back yard he can spit. There he remains suspended in eternity, dazzled to realize that he is now gazing on truth, on the round leaves of the light tree "seized in perpetuity by the unknown." Just as man must advance "implacably in the light" amid ruins, disasters, and the repercussions of war, so the light tree blooms and glows in the yard amid stinkweed and scraps of iron, although unwatered and untended. As in *Paleológhos* king and poet are one, so here the light tree and the poet are identical in their destinies. Here, also, love is the medium: love for woman and love for perfection, for these two are one, both negative and positive aspects, since "the only thing I seek ah is the only thing I do not have." The only thing such a poet ever wants is "what can't be done," the impossible perfection, the impossible truth: only this, the very least, and not the multiformity of the universe. "I wanted the least," he says, "and they punished me with more." On awakening from such vision, on coming out of the dive, out of his suspension beyond time and place, Elýtis is not overwhelmed, as are so many poets, with a haunting despair, for he is pervaded by an intimation that perhaps out of disastrous multiplicity and the suffering this involves is the vision of perfection induced, for "our sufferings are as they should be." The highest beauty is a mingling of pain and pleasure; much toil is needed for the sun to make its daily rounds. In a reference both universal and precisely political, he acknowledges that "the present order is not going to be overthrown." What is to be castigated is the inept cheapening of vision, "Now when no one mourns the nightingales   and all write poems"; or, as he expressed it in an interview in 1973, "Molotov cocktails are heard when nightingales fall silent."

Although the love of liberty permeates all of Elýtis' life and poetry and may be found assimilated into the very texture of his verse as part of the total pattern, it is not in his nature to write directly of political matters, for these have never been an active element in his character, as they have been in such poets as Yánnis Rítsos or Kóstas Várnalis, or in the musician Míkis Theodhorákis, who do and should write of such matters since they have been actively involved from early youth. Elýtis would not deny the validity of such participation or such expression in others, though he believes that much work of this kind tends to become ephemeral if it arises out of intellectual or political conviction alone and not out of aesthetic need. Yet he has made his position plain on several occasions, particularly when ethical or aesthetic matters were at stake: although he accepted the First State Prize in Poetry for *Áxion Estí* in 1960, the Order of the Phoenix for his contribution to Greek letters in 1965, and a Ford Foundation grant in 1972, he refused the Great National Award for Literature of $33,333 offered him in 1973 by those brought into power by the military coup in 1967. Nevertheless, he conceives the role of the artist to be revolutionary and resents all forms of authoritarian rule no matter what their political cast. "All forms of Authority," he said in the same interview, "are of their nature enemies of Art. . . . Basically the artist is for those in authority a suspicious and dangerous person. . . . When I once complained to Picasso, he looked at me, I remember, with his large black eyes, as though surprised, and rebuffed me: 'But aren't you delighted? If the established order were not conservative, how could we possibly be revolutionaries?' Then he burst out laughing; that he might not, I imagine, burst into tears."

Poets throughout the ages have apostrophized the ideal woman, and although Elýtis has felt the pull of this perfection, he has preferred to invoke it within the living experience of love itself and in the palpable body of a young woman. For him the Goddess is not to be halved into Aphrodite Pandemos and Aphrodite Urania, for she is an entity of flesh and spirit, of lust and love. The subtitle of *The Light Tree* is *And the Fourteenth Beauty*, a reference to the belief of the Shiites, a Mohammedan sect, that the Prophet, his daughter Fatima, and their twelve religious leaders, the imams, constitute a holy and prehistoric number, and that all beautiful women are to be found under the aegis of the fourteenth moon. Elýtis was unaware that in Yeats' Lunar Wheel, in *A Vision*, Phase 14 is the phase of the highest possible physical beauty, of Helen of Troy and of his own Aegean girls—the vestibule to Phase 15 of the Full Moon where no human incarnation is possible and where, most likely, all Platonically idealized women, such as Dante's Beatrice, remain forever mesmerized in dream. If the idealized girl is to be invoked, it must not be in sublimation of, but through, the body and the sexual experience itself. Indeed, the excruciating pang of sexual fulfillment, even lust, is not only purified in Elýtis' poems; as a cauterizing experience, it is, itself, also an agent of purification.

Echoes and glimpses of such sexual revelation are to be found in Elýtis' previous poetry, and in "The Other Noah" he says clearly,

"It is time now, I said, for lust to begin its holy career," for all are "to be saved in the Ark of my asceticism," but it pervades and pulses throughout most of the poems in *The Light Tree*, particularly in "On the Republic." In a daydream at dazzling noon, the poet sees a bearded man make a movement as slight but as revolutionary and diverting as that of a railway switcher, a movement as though it were Fate's intention, as he expresses it in the opening of "Monogram," "to shunt the lines of our palm elsewhere." This movement, "which all desired but no one dared," alters the course of previous morality, for it frees from its cage a bird that becomes a woman who spreads out her thighs invitingly on the tiles. Before this gentle gesture of acceptance and invitation, the sinful horses of the Apocalypse and their following mob rush past to be engulfed in the "Gehenna of Paradise." It is typical of Elýtis' use of inversion in these poems that the sexual act should take place in heaven and brim over into life in a wet dream. Moved by the revelation that in Paradise love and lust are an inseparable entity, the poet frenziedly takes up his pen to write "On the Republic," of that utopia where all forms of love and lovemaking may be accepted in their beauty and morality, as diversified as "the various ways birds have of flying little by little   as far as the infinite."

In "The Odyssey," the "small sailor of the garden" of Elýtis' earlier poetry dreams of voyages as his house pitches and tosses like a boat. Passing in reverie through many adventures and traditions of his native land, having as guardians the poet's own Seven Wise Men, themselves a mixture of sensuality and mysticism, the boy indulges in a luxury of the Near East, of an Arabian Night's Entertainment, and as voyeur longs to catch through a keyhole a glimpse of a woman "both the Rose of Espahan and famous Pharizad" as she languidly uncrosses her knees and reveals her "sea urchin   for a moment   in sea-depths unexplored." The mature man understands that the only thing power can do is kill, but not love or lust; that an act is moral or immoral, good or evil, ugly or beautiful only as it is apprehended and created in the mind of man himself; and "that Spring   even Spring   is a product of man." Whatever has once been transmuted into art by love cannot possibly, in Elýtis' estimation, become unethical. Thus, also in "The Girl the North Wind Brought," and again in a moment of oracular revelation induced, this time, by the susurration of olive trees, a

girl approaches flying, an angelic form bringing salvation and resur-
rection. As kindled orbs of light burst behind her, leaving "some-
thing like the elusive signs of Paradise," the young man is in time
to see "the forks between her legs grow wide"; her odor afterwards
reaches him "like fresh bread and wild mountain licorice." It is then
the poet enters a country chapel to light a candle, "because one of
my ideas had become immortal." For Elýtis, the senses and their
delights are holy, hallowed and not hollow.

In all these poems Elýtis further experiments with new forms of
construction and punctuation. Influenced by the practice of sur-
realism, in his early poems, as we have seen, he had almost aban-
doned the normal forms of punctuation or had used them cautiously
when he felt they were utterly necessary. He wished now for the
reader to apprehend his cadences, not only in line lengths, but also
in the rise and fall of the entire stanza; he therefore wrote staves
as one continuous line in which spaces were substituted for punctua-
tion marks, that the reader might know where the poet wished to
pause in the flow of his stanzaic line. This form also permitted Elýtis
—or perhaps itself induced—a looser syntactical and grammatical
structure that became the vehicle of a more relaxed, flowing, and
emotive poetry than any he had previously written. These poems
belong, in kind, to those in *Remorses*, but whereas the latter are
more tightly knit, the images more compact and intellectualized, the
poems in *Light Tree* and *Paleológhos* are more open, their imagery
more expansive and loose, and they rely on apprehension more
by the feeling than by the mind.

IX. MONOGRAM

The poem "Three Times the Truth" is organized in three parts
wherein the last phrases of the first and second parts are repeated
in the opening of the part following. In "Cyclical" the structure
consists of the repetition of an opening dimeter with the second
half of the second line dropped, of another dimeter, of a monometer,
and of a dimeter. This grouping is repeated once, and then the poem
is given cyclical close by the structural repetition of the first dimeter.
In addition, the first lines of each split dimeter are syntactically the
same and are but slightly varied in their content as refrain. In
"Villa Natacha" the poet declares in the first line that he has some-
thing to say, then concludes each of the three sections of the poem

with the phrase "I say" and its revelations. The most complicated structural design, however, is the one that binds the love poem "Monogram" as in an invisible net. Although in content and style it is a love poem, almost a song, and flows with an emotional lyricism, this relatively short poem is as highly schematized as *Axion Estí*. It is as though, knowing that it is almost impossible to write true love poems in our age that are neither maudlin nor sophisticated, Elýtis has tried to give his poem a bone structure that firmly encases and holds upright its pulsing heart and its subsidiary veins and nerves in an anatomy of love. He had noticed that purely by accident in his early poems he tended to group many of his poems and stanzas instinctively in sevens or in multiples of that lucky number. Thus "Windows toward the Fifth Season" is composed of seven stanzas (as are five poems not in this selection, "Waterclocks of the Unknown," "Dionysos," "Seven Nocturnal Septets," "Orion," and "Variations on a Sunray"); the "Lost Second Lieutenant" contains the multiple of fourteen; the "Concert of Hyacinths" and "Pellucid Skies" the multiple of twenty-one. The very nature of their contents make mandatory seven stanzas for "Seven Days for Eternity" and seven parts for the "Genesis" section of *Axion Estí*.

Variation on the number seven reaches extraordinary elaboration in "Monogram." The poem is in seven parts, each consisting of seven lines or of multiples of seven which increase to the central Part IV (containing 49 lines) and decrease analogously to the last part, thus: Part I = 7 lines; II = 21; III = 35; IV = 49; V = 35; VI = 21; VII = 7. Furthermore, although the counterparts have equal numbers of lines, these are arranged in different stanzaic and self-balancing units.

I	II	III	IV	V	VI	VII
3	3	1	11	7	6	2
1	4	7	1	4	4	3
3	7	5	7	3	1	2
7	4	9	11	7	4	7
	3	5	7	3	6	
	21	7	1	4	21	
		1	11	7		
		35	49	35		

In turn, these multiples form in the mind's eye a satisfying harmo-

nious square balanced on one of its corners, and their sums are
7, 21, 35, 49, 35, 21, 7 if added either vertically or horizontally:

```
            7
          7 7 7
        7 7 7 7 7
      7 7 7 7 7 7 7
        7 7 7 7 7
          7 7 7
            7
```

In addition, the line endings of each stanza are arranged in dupli-
cated patterns of dactyl (– ◡ ◡), anapest (◡ ◡ –), or amphibrach
(◡ – ◡). Thus, in Part VI, the first and last stanzas of six lines each
are arranged dactyl, anapest, dactyl, dactyl, anapest, dactyl. The
second and fourth stanzas, of four lines each, are arranged anapest,
anapest, amphibrach, anapest; and the middle stanza, which of course
has no counterpart, is a self-balancing amphibrach (◡ – ◡). If at
times the duplicate stanzas do not at first glance seem to have com-
parable metrical endings, as in stanzas one and three of Part I, an-
other pattern will appear if a line is drawn through the accented
syllables:

Thus, in the five-stanza construction of Part II, the middle stanza of
seven lines contains its own inner scheme:

Similar schemes are developed throughout the poem, with few
variations. In contrast, although the poem is richly rhymed, includ-
ing inner rhymes, there is no patterned rhyme scheme, except oc-

casionally here and there where it is a result more of accident than of plot. Finally, each of the seven parts contains words or phrases so placed or so repeated that, if threaded together, they form the legend: "I shall mourn always—do you hear me?—for you alone in Paradise." In my translation it was easy enough, of course, to keep to the free-verse line and the stanza lengths, and to thread the legend, but more difficult to rhyme the lines, though I have tried, not to duplicate the original placements, but simply to keep with the poet's general intention. It has been impossible, however, to reproduce the highly complicated metrical endings.

Although the poem receives its title from two reflecting monograms, "M. K.," it is written to the dearly beloved of all seasons. In his essential loneliness the poet hymns a love created not only against a back-drop of Aegean landscape and seascape, of basil, roses, and waterfalls but also against the backdrop of the modern crass and catastrophic world. The very quality of the lovers' innocence and their morality has been created out of a mixture of good and evil; it is the "flower of the thunderstorm," and one that "can never blossom in any other way." Out of his adoration, the poet converts the gold that is the beloved into the cry of the wind, the night, water drops, breathing. But he knows that mankind is not as yet prepared to accept what they have created together—their island, their personal Paradise, their uniqueness, their amoral innocence. The poet can only assuage his loneliness by finding and hymning such a counterpart, without whom he and even Paradise itself are half-complete. Although Elýtis never meant this poem as words for song, it nevertheless readily lends itself to musical composition, not that of the popular song, for which he has written many other lyrics, but that of a more symphonic and complex arrangement.

x. The Sovereign Sun

Believing that poems written exclusively to be sung cannot stand alone without their musical accompaniment, Elýtis has only recently yielded to pressure and gathered them in book form, *The Ro of Eros* (1972). This contains seven groups of songs, two of them translations from Brecht and Lorca, four consisting of seven songs each, and the title poem of the multiple twenty-eight. Two of these groups have been set to music, *Small Cyclades* by Míkis Theodhorákis, and *Sea Clover* by Línos Kókotos. Some of his other poems, not in-

41

tended for song, have nevertheless been given musical settings, among them parts of *Áxion Estí* by Theodhorákis; parts of *Sun the First* by Yánnis Markópoulos; and *The Lost Second Lieutenant*, one version by Nótis Mavroudhís, and another by Marínos Mitéllas of Cyprus.

Elýtis began *The Sovereign Sun* as another of these compositions, for Mános Hadzidhákis, but after his long apprenticeship in this form he saw that this particular song had evolved and become self-sustaining poetry based on popular form—something to which W. H. Auden has accustomed the English-speaking world—and published it in book form regardless of a possible musical synthesis. He based its hexameter lines on the meters of several folk songs, and the basic tetrameter lines on a nursery rhyme sung to him by a friend. Superstitiously, he kept to a cast of seven characters. Although by no means comparable to his formal poetry, the result is a charming bittersweet song worthy of being placed as a coda to all of Elýtis' compositions on the Sun, or of lightly complementing his second book, *Sun The First*. His maturity has permitted him to play mockingly yet seriously with some of his most basic themes in the teasing and lilting strains of the nursery rhyme. If I have chosen to entitle the selected poems in this book with its name, I have done so in the spirit of those Renaissance painters who in their own titles picked out minor details for emphasis (e.g., "Man with a Glove" or "Woman with a Pink"), and because the sun is the still center around which Elýtis' imagination revolves.

Beaming benignly from its illusionary orbit high above the earth, the Sun announces that Greece is the land he is most enamored of, with its yellow fields of grain, its emerald seas, its dolphin-riding boys, its naked girls, its daffy roosters. A Chorus of Greek Women reply that this is not the land they know, for theirs is one of poverty and hardship where their sons are regularly sent off to be killed in war, where "every full-grown olive tree / costs an entire family." From his mandatorily lofty position, the Sun immediately sends his Four Winds to scour the earth and to investigate. The Winds report that Greece is indeed a land of sorrow as well as a Paradise. The Sun then broods on the paradoxical character of the land he has adopted as his own. He acknowledges its poverty and sufferings, its oppression by those in power; yet he marvels on the contradictory nature of its people—their whims and caprices, their love of their land

and their departure from it in exile, their tendency toward rebellion and tyranny both, their castigation of their great men. Nevertheless, from his universal yet vulnerable perspective, he thrusts these evils and paradoxes under his fiery millstone and informs mankind that even he, the Sun, must pay most dearly for his own light; that nothing is achieved without trouble and tribulation; that one must "give and take" of Paradise; that the only possible method is to persevere, to endure, to meet "tyrannies tormentors killers and murderers" and "put them to the grindstone for our future years," to have optimistic faith that ultimately justice and freedom will prevail; that evil itself is forced by necessity to come to good, for

> evil itself does bring to birth the blesséd day
> and every narrow lane must lead to the broad highway.

The poem ends with an apostrophe to Greece as a Crazy Boat that since ancient times has weathered stormy elements throughout the centuries both on land and sea, plunging with crazy optimism through all catastrophes. Although at times it is manned by plotting and scheming sailors, by naïve boatswains and unworthy captains, the poet declares:

> we've sailed for years on end, and still we've kept afloat
> we've changed a thousand skippers on this balmy boat.

The Sun now knows that it must receive into its fiery and purifying embrace the evils of this world it so dearly loves, but that such kindling serves only to make it burn and glow with a more intense flame, a transcendental light of the spirit. To the women who weep over their poverty and their sons despoiled by war, the Sun replies compassionately:

> wherever dark and gloom is woven and spun all day
> turn into small small suns, my dears, and grind away.

In the final section of *The Saviors of God,* Kazantzákis likens the universe to a tree of fire and then exclaims: "Amidst the smoke and flames, reposing on the peak of the conflagration, immaculate, cool, and serene, I hold that final fruit of flame, the Light." And so Elýtis, amid the translucent branches of his own Light Tree, gathers under its blazing shadow all he has loved or transmuted into love: his country and her sorrows; her Aegean boys and girls; and the transubstantiation of evil into goodness, into a new and higher morality, into justice. The duty of the poet, Elýtis once said, is "to cast drops of light into the darkness." In this he has succeeded, for all his poems may now be judged to be a metaphysics of light, the refulgence of a Sovereign Sun.

ORIENTATIONS

Départ dans l'affection et le bruit neufs
Rimbaud

OF THE AEGEAN

Love
The archipelago
And the prow of its foam
And the seagull of its dream
On its highest mast the sailor waves
A song

Love
Its song
And the horizons of its voyage
And the echo of its nostalgia
On love's wettest rock the betrothed awaits
A ship

Love
Its ship
And the freedom from care of its etesian winds
And the jib of its hope
On its highest undulation an island rocks
The homecoming

THE GIRLS WHO TROD ON THE FEW

The girls who trod on the few
Enlarged words of the sun
Laughed! And what movement
On the white lilac shrubs
On the foliage that unsuspectingly
Covered the wicked deeds of shadows
The secret nuptial waterdrops

Dreams newly married! Time does not disclaim them
And in its swansdown they find their image.

BREASTING THE CURRENT
Breasting the current
Fish that seek translucency in another climate
Hand that believes in nothing

I am not today as I was yesterday
The weather vanes have taught me to feel
I dissolve the nights and turn joys inside out
I scatter oblivion by opening a dovecote
Leaving by the back door of the sky
Without a word in my glance
Like a boy who hides a carnation
In his hair.

ADOLESCENCE OF DAY
Adolescence of day first lily of joy
The ancient myrtle flutters its flag
The breasts of skylarks shall open to the light
And a song shall hover in mid-air
Sowing the golden barley of fire
To the five winds

Setting free a terrestrial beauty.

WINDOWS TOWARD THE FIFTH SEASON
I
Do you know the flowing hair that wrote the wind? The glances
that ran parallel with time? The silence that understood itself?

But you are a nocturnal contrivance that delights itself in rainy
confidences. That delights itself in the three-masted opening of the
sea. You are an unachievable circumstance that reigns and sets
when shipwrecked. You are a gaudy catastrophe . . .

Ah! May those elements come that know how to grasp. The waist
of my thoughts will gladden their curving disposition. When rings
ascend as they grow larger, the sudden sky will take on the color
of my penultimate sin

While the last one will be enchanted by these solitary words still.

II

A trampling of feet ends at the edge of hearing. A sieved hurricane rushes into the youthful breast that squanders its incomprehensible radiance

Desire possesses an extremely tall stature and absence burns in its palms.

Desire gives birth to the road on which it wishes to pass. It leaves . . .

And a people of hands ignites toward it a consummation of admirations!

III

How beautiful she is! She has taken on the form of that thought which feels her when she feels it devoted to her . . .

IV

My summer abandonments have hidden themselves in ageless vineyards. A billowing wave of dreams drew back and left them there and did not question. In their deaf nets a swarm of honeybees swirled their buzzing. Mouths matched with colors and flew out of flowers. Early morning waters ceased their nocturnal their unsullied speech.

It was as though one knew nothing any more.

And yet behind this small neglected mountain a sentiment exists. It has neither consciousness nor tears.

It does not leave it does not return.

V

An invisible net restrains the sound that puts many truths to sleep. Amid the oranges of its late afternoon, doubt glides. A mouth blows unconcernedly. Its holiday makes desired surfaces shine. One may even believe in himself. May feel the voluptuous pleasure in the pupils of his eyes;

Of his eyes that flow down love's back. And they find their virginal immodesty within the translucent coolness of my most nocturnal grasses.

VI

A gazelle makes the mountain ridge run. You do not know a thing and this is why the distance is so clear. And if ever you learn, the rain that shall drench you will turn sad.

Run away gazelle! O desire close to your salvation, run away life, like a mountain ridge.

VII

Legends suckled the vegetations of this age that lifts up lemon and bitter-orange trees to the astonishment of my eyes. What would happiness have been with its unachievable body if it had become entangled in the flirtations of these green confidences? Two arms are waiting. An entire earth supports itself on their elbows. An entire poetry on their expectation. Beyond the hill is a footpath cut by the fresh footfall of that diaphanous maiden. She had departed from the early morning of my eyes (while eyelids had fulfilled their sun's favor) she had hidden behind the shadow of my desire—and when a wish went to make her his, she vanished blown by affectionate winds whose protection was luminous. The footpath fell in love with the hill that now finally knows the secret well.

Come then remote disappearance! There is nothing the embraces of gardens desire more. In the touch of your palms the fruit will repose that hovers now without purpose. In the translucent abutment of your body's stature, trees will find the long-lived fulfillment of their whispered isolation. In your first freedom from care herbs will multiply like hopes. Your presence will cool the dew.

Then you will open within me fans of sensations. Tears of conscience, precious stones, arrivals and absences. And when the sky runs under the bridges of our woven hands, and when the most precious calyxes match our cheeks, we shall create the form of love lacking from these visions

It is then we shall give

To the ritual of difficult dreams a sure restoration.

THE CONCERT OF
HYACINTHS

THE CONCERT OF HYACINTHS

I

Stand a little closer to silence, and gather up the hair of this night who dreams her body is naked. She has many horizons, many braids, and a fate that untiringly burns each time its fifty-two papers. Afterward she begins again with something else—with your hand, to which she gives pearls that it may find a desire, an island sleep.

Stand a little closer to silence and take in your arms the huge anchor that holds dominion over the sea-depths. In a little while it will be among the clouds. And you will not understand, but you will weep, you will weep that I may kiss you and when I go to open up a crack in falsehood, a small azure skylight in drunkenness, you will bite me. O young jealous girl of my soul, shadow who gives birth to music under the moonlight

Stand a little closer by my side.

II

Here—amid the precocious whispering of desires, you felt for the first time the painful happiness of living. Huge and ambiguous birds tore through the virginities of your worlds. On a spread bedsheet swans gazed on their future songs and from every fold of night set forth by tossing their dreams in the waters, identifying their existence with the existence of the embraces they were waiting for.

Yet the footsteps that did not erase their forests but stopped in the azure nook of the sky and your eyes—what were they seeking? What star-studded sin approached the throbbing of your despair?

Neither the lake, nor its sensitivity, nor the inflammable phantom of two agreeing hands were ever worthy of confronting such a rosy disturbance.

III

Embryo of a more luminous happiness—day carved with difficulty on the traces of the unknown.

The more a tear is paid the more it eludes the sun.

And you chew your hours like oleander and become the omen of a tender voyage into immortality.

IV

Five swallows—five words whose destination is you. Every brilliance closes over you. Before you are simplified into grass you leave your shape on the rock that aches as it flutters its flames inwardly. Before you become a taste of loneliness you enwrap thyme with memories.

And I, I arrive always straight to absence. A sound pretends to be a brook and whatever I say, whatever I love remains untouched in its shadows. Innocencies and pebbles in the depths of a translucency. Sensation of crystal.

V

As you pass and take the swansdown of your age you are named princess. Water shines in a small palm. All the world confuses its days and in the midst of its drunkenness plants a bunch of hyacinths. From tomorrow on you will become the official stranger of my secret pages.

VI

Amid these trees that shall survive your lucid face. The embrace that will move its coolness elsewhere in this simple manner. The world that will remain engraved there.

Oh the closed words that remained in the rinds of hopes, in the shoots of newcut branches of an ambitious day—the closed words that embittered their counterparts and became the Prides.

VII

Deep emotion. Leaves tremble, living together and living separately on poplar trees that portion out the wind. Before your eyes were, this wind existed that liberates these memories, these pebbles —the chimeras! The hour is fluid and you implant yourself upon it, full of thorns. I think of those who never accepted lifeboats. Who love the light under the eyelids, who as sleep reaches its zenith study their open hands sleeplessly.

And I want to close those circles your own fingers opened, to adjust the sky upon them that their ultimate word may never be another.

Speak to me; but speak to me of tears.

VIII

In the sea-depths of music the same things follow you, trans-substantiated. Life everywhere imitates itself. And holding phosphorus in your palm, you circulate motionless amid the filaments of enormous hazard. And your hair watered in the Ninth bends memories and threads vowels on the last pediment of twilight.

Take care! The voice you once forgot now blossoms on your breast. This coral that ignites alone is the vow to which you never consented. And the great fire that would have consumed you is this light dizziness that binds you with a nuance of agony to the last extremities of violets.

In the sea-depths of music we voyage together . . .

IX

I never did anything else. I took you the way you took unused nature and then worked it twenty-four times in the forests and the seas. I took you amid that same shuddering that turned words over and left them there like open and irreplaceable seashells. I took you as companion in the lightning, in awe, in my instinct. Because of this, every time I change day, wringing my heart to the nadir, you leave and disappear, conquering your presence, creating a divine solitude, a turbulent and incomprehensible happiness.

I did nothing else but what I found and imitated in You!

X

Once again amid the cherry trees, your rare lips. Once again amid the vegetable swings, your ancient dreams. Once again in your ancient dreams, the songs that flame up and vanish. Amid these that flame up and vanish, the warm secrets of the world. The secrets of the world.

XI

Aloft on the tree of white voyages, your matutinal body slaked with mainsails, you unfold the naked sea that takes and gives its life to the glittering seaweed. The distance shines and far away a white vapor wrings its heart as it scatters a thousand tears. It is you then who forget Love in the shallow waters, in the underseas of hope. You who forget flames at the height of noon. Who in every multicolored word force the vowels, collecting their honey in fruitbowls.

When the leaf of day returns and you find yourself suddenly a blond and sunburnt girl before this marble hand that shall be the guardian of the centuries, remember at least that boy alone in the rage of the sea who was ambitious to spell out the incomparable beauty of your beauty. Then cast a stone in the navel of the sea, a diamond into the justice of the sun.

XII

Take with you the light of hyacinths and baptize it in the well-spring of day. Thus near your name the legend shall shudder and my hand, conquering the cataclysm, will come out with the first pigeons. Who will first encounter this rustling, who will become worthy enough to feel it near him, who is he who will pronounce you first the way the great sun pronounces the young sprout!

Waves cleanse the world. Everyone searches in his mouth. Where are you I shout and the sea the mountains the trees do not exist.

XIII

Tell me of the cloudtaken hour that conquered you when the thunder preceded my heart. Tell me of the hand that advanced my hand into your sorrow's sojourn in foreign lands. Tell me of the distance and the light and the darkness—the intrusive undulation of a tender and private September.

And scatter the iridescence, wreathe me.

XIV

To return to the island of pumice stone with a forgotten troparion that shall invigorate the bells giving matutinal domes to the memories that have lived most in foreign lands. To air the small gardens outside your heart and afterward to be welcomed again by sorrow itself. Not to feel anything above the austere rocks and yet your form to resemble their hymn suddenly. To be taken up higher and higher by uneven stone stairs and to stand there with your heart beating outside the gate of the new world. To gather laurel and marble for the white architecture of your destiny.

And to be as you were born, the center of the world.

XV

The magnetic needle is endangered. Wherever it may turn it is dazzled by the flaming face of the warmhearted East. Cast then the hyacinths, run on vintagers of foam toward the auspicious six-winged announcement!

The breath of the future beclouds all animate gifts.

XVI

Hide in your forehead the star you wished to find in mourning. And with this proceed and with this suffer beyond the suffering of man. And let the people of others grow humbler. You always know more. And furthermore this is your value and because of this when you raise your flag a bitter color falls on the faces of things that impersonate the titanic world.

XVII

You have learned nothing from whatever was born and from whatever died under desires. You won the confidence of that life which did not tame you, and you continue the dream. What can things say and what things can scorn you?

When you glitter in the sun that on you glides waterdrops, and deathless hyacinths, and silences, I proclaim you the only reality. When you are freed from darkness and return once more with the East, a well, a bud, a sunray, I proclaim you the only reality. When you leave those who are assimilated within nonexistence and offer yourself again as a mortal woman, I awaken in your transformation from the beginning . . .

Do not play any longer. Cast the ace of fire. Break open the human geography.

XVIII

Sunburnt and scintillating girl—lullaby of eyelids on the mythical spaciousness of the world.

It's some time since silence was hurled prone to the wind, it's some time since the wind named its innermost beings one by one.

Now nature is grasped by the hand as it runs beyond there like a child, startling her eyes with an azure tributary, with a skylit foliage, with a new cloud in the shape of lucidity. And I, carving the heart of a walnut tree, fumbling at the sand of the seashore, sounding the boundless distance, have lost the signs that would have given you birth. Where are you when the South Wind exhausts the soul and the Pleiades beckon to night to free the infinite, where are you!

XIX

This bud of fire will open when you baptize your poppy in a different way.

From then on, wherever you may be born again, wherever you may be mirrored, wherever you may shatter your counterpart, my desire shall be found in its April, opening with the same painful ease its seven contemplated flames.

XX

So much light that even the naked line became immortal. The water closed the bays. The solitary tree sketched the distance.

Now it only remains for you to come, you O!, chiseled by the wind's experience, and to replace the statue. It only remains for you to come and turn your eyes toward the sea which at length will be nothing more than your vigorous your unceasing your endless whisper.

It only remains for you to end at the horizons.

XXI

You possess a lethal earth whose pages you skim unceasingly and do not sleep. So many hills you say, so many seas, so many flowers. And your one heart becomes plural, idealizing their quintessence. And wherever you may proceed the distance opens wide, and whatever word you may send to infinity embraces me. Guess, take pains, understand.

On the other side I am the same.

IN THE SERVICE OF SUMMER

ANNIVERSARY

. . . even the weariest river
winds somewhere safe to sea.

I brought my life this far
To this spot that struggles
Always near the sea
Youth on rocks, breast
To breast against the wind
Where a man may go
Who is nothing else but a man
Summing up his green moments
With coolness, the visions of his hearing
With waters, his remorses with wings
Ah, Life
Of a child who becomes a man
Always near the sea when the sun
Teaches him to breathe toward that place where
The shadow of a seagull vanishes.

I brought my life this far
White summation, black total
A few trees and a few
Wet pebbles
Light fingers to caress a forehead
What forehead
Anticipations wept all night and are no more
There is no one
That a free footstep might be heard
That a voice may dawn refreshed
That sterns may splash by quays, inscribing
A name of deeper azure on their horizon
A few years, a few waves
Sensitive rowing
In the bays surrounding love.

I brought my life this far
Bitter gash in the sand that will vanish
—Whoever saw two eyes touching his silence
And mingled with their sunlight enclosing a thousand worlds
Let him remind other suns of his blood
Closer to the light
There is a smile that pays for the flame
But here in this ignorant landscape that fades away
In an open and pitiless sea
Success moults
Whirlwind of feathers
And of moments that have become attached to the earth
Hard earth under the soles of impatient feet
Earth made for vertigo
A dead volcano.

I brought my life this far
A stone pledge to the watery element
Further off than the islands
Lower than the waves
In the neighborhood of anchors
—When keels pass by, splitting some new obstacle
With passion and conquer it
And hope is resplendent with all its dolphins
The sun's gain in a human heart—
The nets of doubt draw up
A figure of salt
Carved with effort
Indifferent, white
That turns toward the sea the void of its eyes
Upholding infinity.

HELEN

With the first drop of rain summer was killed

Those words were drenched that had given birth to starlight

All those words whose unique destination was You!

Where shall we stretch out our hands now that time is no longer
concerned with us

Where shall we rest our eyes now that distant lines have foundered
on the clouds

Now that your eyelids have closed on our landscapes

And we are—as though the fog had gone through us—

Alone all alone surrounded by your dead images.

Forehead on the windowpane, we keep sleepless vigil over this new
grief

It is not death that shall cast us down, for You exist

For a wind elsewhere exists to live in you wholly

To clothe you close by as our hope clothes you from afar

For there exists elsewhere

The greenest of meadows stretching beyond your laughter to the
sun

Telling it in confidence that we shall meet again

No it is not death we shall have to face

But the smallest drop of autumn rain

A blurred emotion

The smell of damp earth in our souls that draw apart the farther
they go.

And if your hand is not in ours

And if our blood is not in the veins of your dreams

The light in the immaculate sky

And music within us invisible O melancholy Lady

O Passer-by—of all things that bind us to this earth still

It is the moist wind the autumnal hour the separation

That appears when night sets out to part us from light

Behind the square window that gazes toward sorrow

That sees nothing

Because it has already become an invisible music a flame in the
fireplace

A chiming of the great clock on the wall
Because it has already become
A poem a verse followed by another verse
A sound parallel with rain tears words
Words unlike all others, but even these have but one destination:
   You!

ODE TO SANTORINI

You rose out of the entrails of thunder
Shuddering amid the repentent clouds
Bitter stone, tested, arrogant
You wanted the sun for your first witness
That you might together confront the perilous radiance
That you might sail out to sea with a cross-bearing echo

Sea-awakened, arrogant
You erected a breast of stone
Speckled by the inspiration of the South Wind
That pleasure might engrave its entrails there
That hope might engrave its entrails there
With fire with lava with smoke
With words that try to convert the infinite
You gave birth to the voice of day
You erected aloft
On the green and rosy ranges of air
The bells struck by the mountainous mind
Glorifying the birds in the light of mid-August

Beside the roaring, beside the anguish of foam
From out the eucharistics of sleep
When night was roaming through a desolation of stars
Searching for the baptismal cross of dawn
You felt the joy of birth
You leapt first into the world
Born to the purple, risen from the sea
You sent as far as the distant horizons
The blessing that grew up by the insomnias of the sea
That it might fondle the hair of the fifth dawn

Queen of Aegean wings and pulses
You found with words that try to convert the infinite
With fire with lava with smoke
The large lines of your destiny

Now justice opens up before you
Black mountains float in the luminosity
Desires prepare their craters
In the heart's tormented land
And a new earth prepares itself from the laboring of hope
That it may walk there with eagles and banners
On a morning filled with iridescences,
The race that invigorates dreams
The race that sings in the sun's arms

O maiden, summit of wrath
Naked form risen from the sea
Open the brilliant gates of man
That all the land may smell fragrantly of health
That sentiment might sprout into a thousand colors
Fluttering in the open sky
And that freedom might blow from every direction

In the proclamation of the wind, flash out
That new and perpetual beauty
When the three-hour sun rises aloft
Totally blue, playing the harmonica of Creation.

MARINA OF THE ROCKS

On your lips there is a taste of storm—But where have you
    wandered
All day long with the hard reverie of stone and sea
An eagle-bearing wind stripped the hills bare
Stripped your desire to the bone
And the pupils of your eyes seized the relay-rod of the Chimera
And lined memory with traceries of foam!
Where has it gone, the familiar slope of childhood's September
Where on red earth you played, gazing below
On the deep thickets of other girls
On corners where your friends left armfuls of rosemary

—But where have you wandered
All night long with the hard reverie of stone and sea
I would tell you to keep trace in the unclothed water of all its
    luminous days
To lie on your back rejoicing in the dawn of all things
Or to wander again in fields of yellow
With a clover of light on your breast, O Heroine of Iambic

On your lips there is a taste of storm
And a dress crimson as blood
Deep within the summer's gold
And the hyacinth's aroma—But where have you wandered

Descending toward the shores, the pebbled bays
Where you found a cold salty seagrass
But deeper still a human emotion that bled
And opened your arms in surprise, calling its name
Lightly ascending to the limpidity of the underseas
Where your own starfish gleamed

Listen, the Word is the prudence of the aged
And Time a frenzied sculptor of men
And the sun stands above it, a beast of hope
And you, much closer, embrace a love
With a bitter taste of storm on your lips

You may no longer count on another summer, O seablue to the bone
That rivers might turn in their courses
To carry you back to their mothers
That you might kiss other cherry trees again
Or ride the horses of the Northwest Wind

Pillared on rock without yesterday or tomorrow,
On the dangers of rock, wearing the headdress of the storm
You shall say farewell to your enigma.

AGE OF BLUE MEMORY

Olive groves and vineyards as far as to the sea
Red fishing boats farther still to memory
Golden cricket husks of August in a midday sleep
With shells or seaweed. And that boat's hull
Newly built, green, that in the water's peaceful embrace still reads:
The Lord Will Provide

Like leaves like pebbles the years went by
I remember the young men, the sailors, leaving
And painting the sails in their hearts' image
They sang of the four corners of the horizon
They wore the north winds tattooed on their chests

What was I looking for when you came painted with the sunrise
The age of the sea within your eyes
And on your body the sun's vigor—what was I looking for
Deep within sea-caverns amid spacious dreams
Where the emotions foamed of a wind
Anonymous and blue, engraving on my chest its sea emblem

With sand on my fingers, I would close my fingers
With sand in my eyes, I would clench my fingers
This was torment—
It was April, I remember, when I felt for the first time your human
    weight
Your human body of clay and corruption
As on our first day on earth
It was the festival of the amaryllis—But you suffered, I remember,
The wound on the bitten lip was deep
And deep the nailmark on the skin where Time is forever engraved

I left you then

And a thundering wind swept up the white houses
The white emotions freshly washed
On a sky that illumined all with a smile

Now I shall keep beside me a jug of immortal water
A form of freedom's ravaging wind
And those hands of yours where Love shall be tormented
And that shell of yours where shall echo the Aegean.

MELANCHOLY OF THE AEGEAN

What coherence of soul amid the halcyons of the afternoon!
What windcalm amid the cries of distant shores!
The cuckoo-bird amid the handkerchief of trees
And the mystic moment of the fishermen's supper
And the sea that with its accordion plays
The distant longing of a woman
The beautiful woman who bared her breasts
When memory entered the nests
And lilacs showered the sunset with fire!

With a caïque with sails of the *Madonna*
They left, and with the well-wishes of the winds
All those who loved the lilies' sojourn in foreign fields
But see how night here has poured out warbling sleep
Like gurgling hair on the gleaming necks
Of vast white seashores
And how the dust of maiden dreams
Fragrant with spearmint and basil
Was scattered and brimmed on high
By the golden sword of Orion!

On three crossroads where the ancient sorceress stood
Setting the winds aflame with dry thyme
Lightly stepped the slender shadows
Each holding a jug immured with muted water
Easily as though they were going into Paradise
And from the crickets' prayers that foamed on all the fields
The beautiful ones emerged with the moon's skin
To dance on the midnight threshing floor . . .

O signs drifting in the depths
Of a pool that holds up a mirror
O seven small lilies that glitter

When the sword of Orion wheels round again
It shall find the bread of poverty under the lamp
But a soul on the glowing embers of the stars
It shall find huge hands branching into the infinite
Desolate seaweed, the lastborn children of the seashore
And years, green precious stones

O green stone—what storm-diviner saw you
Halting the light at the birth of day
Light at the birth of the world's two eyes!

SHAPE OF BOEOTIA

Here where a desolate glance blows on stones and the
    deathless cacti
Here where the footsteps of time resound in the deep
Where the enormous clouds open into golden six-winged cherubim
Above the metope of the sky
Tell me from where has eternity risen
Tell me what is the bruise that hurts you
And what the destiny of the humble tapeworm

O earth of Boeotia brightened by the wind

What has become of the orchestra of nude hands below the palaces
The mercy that rose like the smoke of holiness
Where are the gates with archaic birds that sang
And the clang of metal that daybroke the terror of the people
When the sun entered like a triumph
When fate writhed on the lance of the heart
And the civil strife of birdsong raged
What has become of the immortal March libations
Of Greek traceries on the watery grass

Brows and elbows were wounded
Time from too much sky rolled crimson
Men advanced
Laden with lament and dream

Acrid shape! Ennobled by the wind
Of a summer storm that leaves its flame-gold traces
On the lines of hills and eagles
On the lined palms of your destiny

What can you face and what can you wear
Dressed in the music of grass and how do you proceed
Amid the sage and the heather
Toward the final reach of the arrow

69

On this red earth of Boeotia
Amid the desolate musical march of rock
You shall ignite the golden sheafs of fire
You shall uproot the evil crop of memory
You shall leave a bitter soul in the wild mint!

BEAUTIFUL GIRL IN A GARDEN

You wake on the waterdrop of noon
At the beginning of the trees' song
Oh how beautiful you are
With your joyful hair flowing free
And with the open fountain from which you came
So I might hear that you live and go walking by!

Oh how beautiful you are
Running with the skylark's bloom
Around the eglantine that blows on you
Like a sigh blowing on fluffy down
With a large sun in your hair
And with a honeybee in the brilliance of your dance

Oh how beautiful you are
With the new earth you ache for
From the root to the summit of shadows
Amid nets of eucalyptus trees
With half the sky in your eyes
And the other half in eyes you love

Oh how beautiful you are
As you awaken the mill of winds
And lean your nest to the left
That so much love might not go lost
That not even one shadow may complain
To the Greek butterfly-girl you inflamed

High up with your morning delight
Filled with the grasses of the East
Filled with birds for the first time heard
Oh how beautiful you are
Casting the waterdrop of day
On the beginning of the trees' song!

THE MAD POMEGRANATE TREE

an early-morning question mood of high spirits à perdre haleine

In these whitewashed courtyards where the South Wind blows
Whistling through vaulted arcades, tell me is it the mad
  pomegranate tree
That frisks in the light scattering her fruit-laden laughter
With a wind's caprice and murmuring, tell me is it the mad
  pomegranate tree
That quivers with newborn foliage at early dawn
Unfolding all her colors on high with a triumphant tremor?

When in the meadows the naked girls awaken
To harvest with blond hands the green clover,
Roaming on the borders of sleep, tell me is it the mad pomegranate
  tree
That unsuspectingly places lights in their fresh-woven baskets
That overbrims their names with birdsong, tell me
Is it the mad pomegranate tree that skirmishes with the world's
  cloudy skies?

On the day that enviously adorns itself with seven varied feathers
Encircling the eternal sun with a thousand blinding prisms
Tell me is it the mad pomegranate tree
That seizes on the run a horse's mane of a hundred lashes,
Never sad and never complaining, tell me is it the mad pomegranate
  tree
That shouts aloud the newborn hope now dawning?

Tell me is it the mad pomegranate tree that greets us afar
Tossing a leafy handkerchief of cool fire
A sea about to give birth to a thousand and one ships
To waves that arise a thousand and one times and go
To untrodden shores, tell me is it the mad pomegranate tree
That creaks the rigging aloft in the translucent air?

High up aloft with the blue grapeclusters that glow and revel
.Arrogantly, filled with peril, tell me is it the mad pomegranate tree
That in the world's midst shatters with light the demon's inclement
    weather,
That spreads from end to end the crocus collar of day
Richly embroidered with sown songs, tell me is it the mad
    pomegranate tree
That hastily unravels the silks of day?

Amid the petticoats of April first and the cicadas of mid-August
Tell me, she who frolics, she who rages, she who allures,
Shaking out of all menace its black and evil darkness
Pouring out upon the sun's bosom the giddy birds
Tell me, she who unfolds her wings on the breasts of all things
On the breast of our deepest dreams, is it the mad pomegranate
    tree?

SUN THE FIRST

*Often when I'm speaking of the sun a huge all-crimson rose
becomes entangled in my tongue, and yet it's not possible for
me to stop speaking.*

I KNOW THE NIGHT NO LONGER

I know the night no longer, the terrible anonymity of death
A fleet of stars moors in the haven of my heart
O Hesperos, sentinel, that you may shine by the side
Of a skyblue breeze on an island that dreams
Of me announcing the dawn from its rocky heights
My twin eyes set you sailing embraced
With my true heart's star: I know the night no longer

I know the names no longer of a world that disavows me
I read seashells, leaves, and the stars clearly
Hatred is for me superfluous on the roads of the sky
Unless it is the dream that watches me again
As I walk by the sea of immortality in tears
O Hesperos, under the arc of your golden fire
I know the night no longer that is a night only.

BODY OF SUMMER

A long time has passed since the last rainfall was heard
Above the ants and the lizards
Now the sky burns endlessly
The fruit trees paint their mouths
The pores of the earth very slowly open
And beside the trickling and syllabic waters
A huge plant stares straight into the sun.

Who is this who sprawls on the far beaches
Stretched on his back, smoking the smokesilver olive leaves
Crickets warm themselves in his ears
Ants scurry to work on his chest
Lizards glide in the long grasses of his armpits
And through the seaweed of his feet a wave lightly passes
Sent by that small siren who sang:

"O naked body of summer, burnt
And eaten away by oil and salt
Body of rock and the heart's tremor
Great fluttering in the willow's hair
Breath of basil on the curly groin
Filled with starlets and pine needles
Profound body, vessel of day!"

75

The slow rains come, the pelting hail,
The shores pass by, flogged by the claws of the wintry wind
That with savage billows lowers in the sea-depths
The hills plunge into thick udders of clouds
But behind all this you smile unconcernedly
And find again your deathless hour
As once more you are found on the beaches by the sun
And amid your naked vigor by the sky.

GLITTERING DAY, CONCH OF THE VOICE

Glittering day, conch of the voice that created me
Naked, to walk on my daily Sundays
Amid the welcoming cry of seashores
Blow on the first-known wind
Spread out an affectionate green meadow
On which the sun may roll his head
And light up poppies with his lips
Poppies that proud men will pluck
So there may be no other mark on their naked chests
Than the blood of carefree disdain that erased sorrow
Reaching as far as the memory of freedom

I spoke of love, of the rose's health, the sunray
That alone finds the heart straightway
Of Greece that walks the sea with surety
Of Greece that takes me on voyages always
To naked snow-glorious mountains

I give my hand to justice
Translucent fountain, spring on the mountain summit
My sky is deep and unchanging
Whatever I love is born unceasingly
Whatever I love is always at its beginning.

DRINKING THE CORINTHIAN SUN

Drinking the Corinthian sun
Reading the marble ruins
Striding over vineyard seas
Aiming with my harpoon
At votive fish that elude me
I found those leaves that the psalm of the sun memorizes
The living land that desire rejoices
To open

I drink water, cut fruit
Plunge my hands through the wind's foliage
Lemon trees quicken the pollen of summer days
Green birds cut through my dreams
And I leave, my eyes filled
With a boundless gaze where the world becomes
Beautiful again from the beginning according to the heart's measure.

BELOW, ON THE DAISY'S SMALL
THRESHING FLOOR

Below, on the daisy's small threshing floor
The young honeybees have struck up a crazy dance
The sun sweats, the water trembles
Sesame seeds of fire slowly fall
Tall stalks of corn bend the sunburnt sky

With bronze lips, naked bodies
Scorched on the tinderbox of fervor
Ee! Eee! The carriage drivers pass jouncing by
Horses sink in the oil of descending slopes
Horses dream
Of a cool city with marble troughs
Or of a clovercloud ready to burst
On a hill of slender trees that scalds their ears
On the tambourines of large fields that set their dung to dancing

Beyond in the golden millet tomboys drowse
Their sleep smells of bonfires burning
The sun quivers between their teeth
Nutmeg sweetly drips from their armpits
And a drunken heat haze staggers with heavy strokes
On the heather the everlasting and the sweet-smelling jujube tree.

CHILD WITH THE SKINNED KNEE
Child with the skinned knee
Close-cropped head, dream uncropped
Legs with crossed anchors
Arm of pine, tongue of fish
Small brother of the cloud!

You saw a wet pebble whitening beside you
You heard a reed whistling
The most naked landscapes of which you knew
The most colorful
Deep oh deep the funny walk of the gilthead
High oh high the cap of the small church
And far oh far a ship with red smokestacks

You saw the wave of plants where the hoarfrost
Took its morning bath, the leaf of the prickly pear
The bridge at the turn of the road
But also the savage smile
On the huge buffeting of trees
On the huge solstices of marriage
Where tears drip from the hyacinths
Where the sea urchin unravels the riddles of water
Where stars forecast the storm

Child with the skinned knee
Crazy amulet, stubborn jaw
Airy shorts
Breast of the rock, lily of the water
Gamin of the white cloud!

SAILOR BOY OF THE GARDEN

With a luffing spirit with brine on his lips
With his sailor suit and his red sandals
He clambers up on clouds
Treads on the seaweeds of the sky.
Dawn whistles in her conch
A prow approaches foaming
Angels! Push back your oars
That *Our Lady of the Annunciation* might anchor here!

On the earth below, how he admires the patricians of gardens!
When the sunflower turns its head uncombed
The reservoirs overflow
And *Our Lady of the Annunciation* enters
Naked, dripping foam, with starfish on her forehead
With a wind of clove pinks on her flowing hair
And a crab still tottering on her sunburnt shoulder.

—Godmother of my white birds
My Gorgon Lady of the Annunciation!
What spheres of seablue carnations are your cannons shooting on
    the quay
How many flotillas of shells are your fires sinking
Ah how you bend the palm trees when the southwest wind goes
    crazy
And sweeps up sand and pebbles!

Hopes pass within her eyes
With boats made of cuttlefish bones,
On the three dolphins that leap and dance
Behind her, swollen banners flutter.

—Ah, with what violets, with what lilac shrubs
I would nail—have mercy!—a blessing on your bosom
That you may ordain another destiny for me!
I cannot endure the land
Bitter-orange trees cannot hold me
Let me sail for the open seas with gunfire and monastery bells!

Quickly O my Madonna, quickly
Already I hear a harsh voice high above the battlements
It strikes it strikes on the copper crossbars
It strikes it strikes and grows manly
Her silver ornaments glitter like suns
Ah she commands us—don't you hear her?—
Ah she commands us: Bouboulína!

And the Madonna rejoices the Madonna smiles
How the sea resembles her as it flows so deeply:
—Yes, you stubborn head
Yes, you sailor boy of the garden
In your sleep three three-masted schooners wait for you!

Now with his straw hat askew and his red sandals
With a jackknife in his hand
The sailor boy of the garden goes
And cuts the yellow roses
Slackens the white clouds
Dawn whistles in her conch
Gunpowder bursts in dreams
Easter in the seaweed of the sky!

HALF-SUNKEN BOATS

Half-sunken boats
Wood that swells with pleasure
Winds barefoot winds
On the deafened cobblestone streets
Stony downhill slopes
The mute one, the crazy one
The half-built hope

Great news, bells
The cleansed white wash of the day in the back yard
Skeletons on the seashore
Paints, tar, turpentine
Preparations for the Virgin Mary
Who to celebrate her fiesta hopes
For white sails and small blue flags

And you in the upper gardens
Beast of the wild pear tree
Slender unripe boy
The sun between your thighs
Sniffing the scent
And the young girl on the opposite strand
Slowly burning because of the hydrangeas.

THIS WIND THAT LOITERS

This wind that loiters and gapes in the quince trees
This insect that sucks the grapevines
This stone that the scorpion wears next to its skin
And these wheat-stacks on the threshing floor
That play the giant to small barefoot children

Icons of the Resurrection
On walls that pine trees scratched with their fingers
This whitewash that bears all noons on its back
And the cicadas the cicadas in the ears of trees

Huge summer of chalk
Huge summer of cork
Red sails slanting in the squalls
Bleach-blond creatures on the sea-bottom, sponges
Accordions of the rocks
Sea perch fresh from the fingermarks of the awkward
    fisherman
Proud reefs on the fishing lines of the sun

One, two: no one shall tell us our fate
Three, four: we shall tell the sun's fate ourselves.

WE WALKED IN THE FIELDS ALL DAY

We walked in the fields all day
With our women our suns our dogs
We played we sang we drank water
Fresh as it sprang from the ages

81

In the afternoon we sat for a moment
And looked each other deeply in the eyes
A butterfly flew from our breasts
It was whiter
Than the small white branch at the tip of our dreams
We knew it was never to vanish
That it never remembered what worms it dragged along

At night we lit a fire
And around it we sang:

Fire lovely fire do not pity the logs
Fire lovely fire do not come to ash
Fire lovely fire burn us
                    tell us of life.

It is we who tell of life, we take her by the hands
We look into her eyes that look into our own
And if this that makes us drunk is a magnet, we know it
And if this that gives us pain is misfortune, we have felt it
It is we who tell of life, we go forward
And say farewell to her migrating birds

We come of a good stock.

THE ORANGE GIRL

She became so intoxicated by the sun's juice
That she bowed her head and consented
Slowly slowly to become: the small Orange Girl!

And so while the seven skies glittered with blue
And so while the crystals touched a fire
And so while swallow tails flashed
Angels above were bewildered and girls below
Storks above were bewildered and peacocks below
And all gathered together and all saw her together
And all together called her: the Orange Girl!

Vineshoots and scorpions reel drunkenly the whole world is
    drunk
But the sting of day will not leave pain alone
The dwarf heron says it amid the earthworms
The drip-drop of water says it amid golden moments
And the dew says it to the lips of the good North Wind:

Get up O small small small Orange Girl!
No one knows you as the kiss knows you
Nor does the laughing god know you
Who with his hand open to the flaming glare of the sun
Exposes you naked before his thirty-two winds!

HEROIC AND ELEGIAC SONG FOR THE LOST SECOND LIEUTENANT OF THE ALBANIAN CAMPAIGN

HEROIC AND ELEGIAC SONG FOR THE LOST SECOND LIEUTENANT OF THE ALBANIAN CAMPAIGN

I

There where the sun first dwelt
Where the weather opened with a virgin's eyes
As the air from the shaking of an almond tree snowed
And horsemen blazed up on the tips of vegetation

There where the hoof of a fearless plane tree struck
And a flag fluttered earth and water on high
Where weapons never burdened the backs of men
But all the toil of the sky
All the world shone like a waterdrop
In the morning, at the foot of the mountain

Now, as from the sigh of a god, a shadow enlarges

Now agony stoops with bony hands
Takes and smothers the flowers upon her one by one;
In gorges where waters stopped
The songs lie down famished for joy;
Monk-rocks with cold hair
Silently cut the consecrated bread of desolation.

Winter enters up to the brain. Something evil
Shall flame up. The hair of the horse-mountain grows savage

High up the vultures share the bread crumbs of the sky.

II

Now in the muddy waters an agitation rises;

The wind seized by the foliage
Blows its dust far away
Fruits spit out their pits
Earth hides her stones
Fear digs a hole and scurries into it
In that hour when from the bushes of the sky
The howl of the wolfcloud
Scatters on the hide of the field the tempest's tremors
And then spreads spreads the pitiless snow the snow
And then goes whinnying over the fasting valleys
And then sets men to hailing one another:
Fire or the sword!

For those who set out with fire or the sword
Evil will flame up here. Let the cross despair not
Only let violets say their prayers far from the cross.

III

For them night was a more bitter day
They melted iron, chewed earth
Their god smelled of gunpowder and mulehide

Every thunderbolt was a death astride the air
Every thunderbolt a man smiling on the other side
Of death—and let fate say what it will.

Suddenly the moment missed its mark and found courage
Facing the sun, it threw splinters into it
Binoculars, telemeters, mortars froze!

The air tore as easily as calico.
The stones opened as easily as lungs.
The helmet rolled from his left side . . .

The roots in the earth were startled only for a moment
Then the smoke scattered and the day went timidly
To deceive the tumult from the infernal regions

But the night half-rose like a trodden viper
When death for a moment paused between his teeth
Then suddenly flowed into his pallid fingertips.

IV

He lies down now on his scorched battle-coat
With a halted breeze on his quiet hair
With a twig of forgetfulness on his left ear
He resembles a garden from which the birds have suddenly flown
He resembles a song muzzled in the darkness
He resembles the clock of an angel stopped
Just when the eyelashes said: "So long, boys"
And amazement turned into stone . . .

He lies down on his scorched battle-coat.
The black centuries around him
Bark with the skeletons of dogs at the dreadful silence
And the hours that have become stone pigeons again
Listen with attention;
But laughter was scorched, but the earth was deafened,
But no one heard his very last shriek
All the world was emptied with his last shriek.

Under five cedar trees
With no other candles
He lies on his scorched battle coat;
The helmet empty, the blood muddy,
At his side the half-finished arm
And between his eyebrows—
A small bitter well, fingerprint of fate
A small bitter black-red well
Well where memory grows cold.

Oh do not see oh do not see from where his
From where his life has fled. Do not say how
Do not say how the smoke of the dream rose high
In this way then the one moment In this way then the one
In this way then the one moment abandoned the other
And the eternal sun in this way suddenly left the world.

V

Sun, were you not the eternal one?
Bird, were you not the moment of joy that never rests?
Brightness, were you not the fearlessness of cloud?
And you, garden, music hall of flowers,
And you, curling root, flute of the magnolia tree!

Just as the tree shakes itself in the rain
And the empty body blackens from fate
And a crazy man battles with the snow
And both eyes are on the point of tears—
Why, the eagle asks, where is that brave young man?
And all the eaglets wonder where the brave young man might be!
Why, the mother asks sighing, where is my son?
And all the mothers wonder where the boy might be!
Why, the companion asks, where might my brother be?
And all his companions wonder where the youngest of all might be!
They grasp snow, the fever burns
They grasp the hand and it freezes
They try to bite bread and it drips with blood
They look at the sky far away but it blackens
Why why why why should death not bring us warmth
Why such unholy bread
Why such a sky as this where once the sun dwelt!

VI

He was a handsome lad. On the day of his birth
The mountains of Thrace bent down to reveal
The cheerful wheat on the shoulders of firm earth;
The mountains of Thrace bend down and spat on him
Once on the head, once on the chest, and once amid his crying;
Greeks came with terrible arms
And raised him high in the swaddling clothes of the North Wind . . .
Then the days ran to see who could cast the farthest stone
They bucked and kicked as they rode the young mares
Then morning Strymon rivers rolled
Until gypsy windflowers rang everywhere
And from the ends of the earth
Shepherds of the sea came to take their flocks of jib-sails
To where a sea-cave deeply breathed
To where a great stone sighed.

He was a sturdy lad;
In the arms of bitter-orange girls at night
He would soil the large garments of the stars,
Love was so huge within him
That in wine he drank the flavors of all earth
Joining in dance later with the white-poplar brides
Until dawn heard him and spilled light into his hair
Dawn who with open arms would find him
Scratching the sun on a saddle of two small branches,
Painting the flowers
Or again singing with love a slow lullaby
To the small owls that lay awake all night . . .
Ah what strong thyme was his breath,
What a map of pride his naked chest
Where seas and freedom burst . . .

He was a valiant lad;
With his dull gold buttons and his pistol
With a manly air in his stride
With his helmet, a glittering target
(They reached so easily into his brain
He who had never known evil)
With his soldiers to left and right
And revenge for injustice done before him
—Flame on lawless flame!—
With blood above his eyebrows.
The Albanian mountains thundered
Then they melted snow to wash
His body, silent shipwreck of dawn
And his mouth, small songless bird
And his hands, wide plains of desolation
The Albanian mountains thundered
They did not weep
Why should they weep
He was a valiant lad!

VII

The trees are made of coal which the night cannot inflame
The wind pounces, the wind ravages and rages again.
Nothing. Amid the freezing cold the mountains huddle together
On their knees. And from the gorges howling,
From the heads of the dead the abyss ascends . . .
Not even Pity weeps any more. Like a crazy orphan girl
She wanders aimlessly, wearing on her breast a small cross of twigs
She does not weep. Zoned only by the black Akrokerávnia
She mounts higher and plants a plaque of the moon
That the planets in turning may see their shadows perhaps
And hide their rays
And stop
There in chaos panting, ecstatic . . .

The wind pounces, the wind ravages and rages again
The wilderness tightens her black shawl about her
Crouched behind month-clouds, straining to listen
What is it that strains to listen, cloud-months away?

With the rags of her hair down her shoulders—ah let her be—
Half-candle half-fire a mother weeps—let her be—
In the frozen empty rooms where she wanders, let her be!
Because fate is not anyone's widow
And mothers are made for weeping and men for fighting
Gardens for bringing to bloom the bosoms of girls
Blood to be spent, the surf to crash
And freedom to be born unceasingly like lightning!

VIII

Well then, tell the sun to find a new road
If it wishes to lose nothing of its pride
Now that its native land has darkened on earth;
Or then again with water and earth
Let it bring to an azure birth elsewhere a younger sister, Greece.
Tell the sun to find a new road
Let it face no longer not even a daisy
Tell the daisy to sprout with another virginity
Not to be soiled by fingers that do not become her.

Separate the wild doves from fingers
And let no sound tell of the water's passion
As the sky sweetly blows into an empty shell
Do not send a sign of despair anywhere
But bring from the gardens of gallantry
The rose trees where his spirit shook and tossed
The rose trees where his breathing played
At being the small bride-chrysalis
That changes as many costumes as satin has folds
In the sun, when goldflies are drunken with golddust
And the birds go in haste to hear from the trees
What progeny of what seed erected the famous earth.

IX

Bring him new hands for who shall go now
On high to lullaby the infants of the stars!
Bring him new feet for who shall join now
First in the folk dances of the angels!
New eyes—dear God—for where shall the small lilies
Of the beloved go now to lean and look!
New blood, for with what joyous greeting will they flame up
And mouth, cool mouth of brass and amaranth
For who among the clouds will say now "Your health, boys!"

Daytime, who will defy the peach tree leaves
Nighttime, who will domesticate the green crops
Who will scatter green church lamps in the fields
Or shout courageously, confronting the sun
To wear tempests, astride an invulnerable horse
And become the Achilles of the shipyards!
Who will ascend the black and mythical desolate island
To kiss the pebbles with reverence
And who will sleep
To pass by the Euboeans of dream
To find new hands, feet, eyes
Blood and speech
To implant himself again on the white threshing floor
And to pounce—ah this time—
To pounce with all his holiness on Death!

X

The sun, the sound of brass, and the sacred etesian winds
Vowed on his breast, "Life, may I take joy of you!"
There was no room there for a darker power
Only with light spilled from a laurel bough
And silver from dewdrops, only there the cross
Flashed like lightning as Greatness was dawning
And Goodness appeared with sword in hand
To say from within his eyes and their banners "I live!"

Good-day there river who would at daybreak see
A similar child of God with a twig of pomegranate
In his teeth, perfuming himself with your waters;
And good-day to you, wild medlar tree who waxed manly
Whenever Androútsos wished to enter his dreams!
And you, small spring of midday that reached up to his feet
And you, O maiden who were his Helen
Who were his bird his Madonna his Pleiades
For if the love given by a man should ring out
In life but once only, lighting up
From star to star the hidden firmaments,
Then everywhere always the godly echo shall reign
To adorn the woods with the small hearts of birds
And the words of poets with lyres of jasmine

And torment secret evil wherever it may be—
And flaring up, torment secret evil wherever it may be.

XI

Those who committed evil—because sorrow
Had taken their eyes, went staggering
Because terror had taken
Their sorrow, vanished in the black cloud.
Back! and with feathers no longer on their foreheads
Back! and with nails no longer on their feet
There where the sea undresses vineyards and volcanoes
To the fields of their country again, and with the moonplow.
Back! to the places where the houndlike fingers
Sniff out the flesh and where the storm lasts
As long as white jasmine on the summer of women!

Those who committed evil—a black cloud took them
They had no life to back them up with fire and cold waters
With lamb, wine and shooting of guns, a spit, a cross of vine-twigs
They had no grandfather of oak and of frenzied wind
In ambush for eighteen days and nights
With embittered eyes;
A black cloud took them—they did not have an uncle
To back them up who fired cannon, a father who packed powder
A mother who had slain with her own hands
Or a mother's mother who with naked breast
Gave herself in dancing to the liberation of Death!

They who committed evil—a black cloud took them
But he who faced it on the roads of the sky
Ascends alone now and bazing with light.

XII

With a morning stride on the growing grass
He ascends alone and blazing with light . . .

Flower tomboys wave to him secretly
And speak to him in high voices that turn to mist on the air
Even the trees bend toward him lovingly
With their nests thrust into their armpits
With their branches dipped in the oil of the sun.
Miracle—what a miracle, low on the earth
White tribes with azure plowshares cut the fields
Mountain ranges flash like lightning far away
And farther away the inaccessible dreams of springtime mountains!

He ascends alone and blazing with light
So drunk with light that his heart shows through
And the true Olympos can be seen amid the clouds
And the hosannahs of his comrades in the air around . . .
The dream now throbs more swiftly than blood
On the banks of footpaths the animals gather
They rasp like crickets and seem to be speaking
All the world is in truth enormous
A giant who fondles his children.

Bells of crystal are ringing far away
Tomorrow, tomorrow they say: the Easter of the Sky!

XIII

Bells of crystal are ringing far away—

They tell of him who burned in life
Like the honeybee in the upsurge of wild thyme;
Of the dawn that drowned on earthen breasts
Though it was announcing a brilliant day;
Of the snowflake that flashed in the brain and vanished
When the whistling of bullets was heard far away
And the Albanian partridge flew high in lamentation.

They tell of him who was not given time to weep
For his deep longing for the Love of life
When the wind gathered in strength far away
And birds crowed on the beams of the ruined mill,
Of the women who drank wild music
Standing erect by the window and squeezing their handkerchiefs
Of the women who made desperation despair
Waiting for a black mark there where the field begins
And then for heavy hoofbeats outside the threshold
They tell of his warm and uncaressed head
Of his large eyes where life was contained
So deeply it may never get out again!

XIV

Now the dream in the blood throbs more swiftly
The truest moment of the world rings out:
Liberty,
Greeks show the way in the darkness:
L I B E R T Y
For you the eyes of the sun shall fill with tears of joy.

Rainbow-beaten shores fall into the water
Ships with open sails voyage on the meadows
The most innocent girls
Run naked in men's eyes
And modesty shouts from behind the hedge
Boys! there is no other earth more beautiful

The truest moment of the world rings out!

With a morning stride on the growing grass
He is continually ascending;
Around him those passions glow that once
Were lost in the solitude of sin;
Passions flame up, the neighbors of his heart;
Birds greet him, they seem to him his younger brothers
Men hail him, they seem to him his companions
"Birds my dear birds, this is where death ends!"
"Comrades my dear comrades, this is where life begins!"
The dew of heavenly beauty glistens in his hair.

Bells of crystal are ringing far away
Tomorrow, tomorrow, tomorrow: the Easter of God!

from AXION ESTI

Many a time they have afflicted me from my youth:
yet have they not prevailed against me.

Psalm 129

from GENESIS
GENESIS III
But before hearing wind or music
as I set out to find a clearing
(ascending an endless red tract of sand
and erasing History with my heel)
I struggled with my bedsheets   What I was looking for
was as innocent and tremulous as a vineyard
as deep and unmarked as the sky's other face
And a bit of soul within the clay
Then he spoke and the sea was born
And I saw and marveled
And in its midst he sowed small worlds in my image and likeness:
Steeds of stone with manes erect
and amphorae serene
and the slanting backs of dolphins
Íos   Sériphos   Síkinos   Mílos
"Every word a swallow
to fetch you spring in the midst of summer," he said
And ample the olive trees
to sift the light through their fingers
as it spreads softly over your sleep
and so ample the cicadas
that you do not heed them
as you do not heed the pulse in your hand
but scarce the water
that you may hold it a God
and understand the meaning of its voice
and alone the tree
without a flock of its own
that you may take it for friend
and know its exact name
sparse the earth beneath your feet
that you may have nowhere to spread root
and must reach for depth continually
and broad the sky above
that you may read the infinite yourself

THIS
small, this great world!

GENESIS IV
"And you must see and accept this world,"
      he said: "Look!" And my eyes cast the seed
      as they raced even faster than rain
      over thousands of untrodden acres
Sparks taking root in darkness and jets of sudden water
            The silence I was clearing to implant
            germ-cells of sound and golden shoots of oracles
The pick-axe still in my hand
      I saw the large shortlegged plants, turning their faces
      some barking some sticking out their tongues:
            There the asparagus there the chick-pea
            there the curly parsley
            there the ginger and the geranium
            there the snakeroot and the fennel
The cryptic syllables through which I strove to articulate my
      identity
"Well done," he said to me, "you know how to read
and there is much you shall learn
      if you probe deeply into the Insignificant
      And a day will come when you'll take on assistants
            Remember:
            the double-edged Zephyr
            the dark-slaughtering pomegranate
            the blazing fleetfoot kisses"
And his words vanished like a fragrance
The ninth hour, the partridge, struck the profound heart of euphony
            the houses stood in solidarity
            small and square with white arches
            and door shutters the color of bluing
      Under the grapevine arbor
      there I sat in reverie for hours
      with tiny, very tiny twitterings
      croakings, cluckings, distant cooings:
            There the baby pigeon there the stork
            there the night owl
            the whippoorwill and the water hen

and the wasp was there too
and what is called the Virgin's colt
The shore with my thighs naked in the sun
　　and two seas again on either side
　　and a third in between—trees of lemon, lime and tangerine—
　　and the other northwest wind with its own channel aloft
　　changing the sky's ozone
　　　　　Lower down on the seafloor of leaves
　　　　　the smooth shingle
　　　　　the small ears of flowers
　　　　　and the impatient young sprout and all are

THIS
small, this great world!

GENESIS V

Then I came to understand the sea-murmur
and the long endless whispering of trees
　　I saw red jugs lined up on the mole
　　and closer by the wooden window shutter
　　where I lay sleeping on my side
　　　　　the North Wind spoke in a louder tone
　　　　　And I saw
girls as beautiful and naked and smooth as pebbles
with a bit of black in the nook of their thighs
and that abundant and luxurious spread of it
along the shoulder blades
　　　　　some erect blowing the Conch Shell
　　　　　and others writing with chalk
　　　　　words strange and enigmatic:
　　ROES, ESA, ARIMNA
　　NUS, MORIMLATITY, YLETIS
　　　　　small cries of birds and hyacinths
　　　　　or other words of July
At the stroke of eleven
　　five fathoms deep
　　perch gudgeon sea-bream
　　with enormous gills and short tails astern

Rising higher I found sponges
and starfish
and slender silent anemones
and higher still at the water's lips
pink limpets
and half-open wing-shells and saltweed
"Precious words," he said, "ancient oaths
preserved by Time and the sure hearing of distant winds"
And close by the wooden window shutters
where I lay sleeping on my side
I pressed the pillow tight against my chest
and my eyes filled with tears
I was in the sixth month of my loves
and in my entrails stirred a precious seed

THIS
small, this great world!

from THE PASSIONS
PSALM I

This then is I
created for young girls and the islands of the Aegean;
    lover of the roebuck's leap
and neophyte of the olive trees;
    sun-drinker and locust-killer.
This is I face to face
    with the black shirts of the resolute
and the empty womb of the years that aborted
    its children, the seductive cries!
Air unleashes the elements and thunder attacks the mountains.
    Fate of the innocent, you are here, alone again at the Pass!
At the Pass I opened my hands
    at the Pass I emptied my hands
and saw no other riches, and heard no other riches
    but cold fountains pouring out
Pomegranates or Zephyrs or Kisses.
    Each with his own weapons, I said:
At the Pass I'll deploy my pomegranates
    at the Pass I'll post my zephyrs guard
I'll set the old kisses free, made holy by my longing!
    Air unleashes the elements and thunder attacks the mountains.
Fate of the innocent, you are my own fate!

PSALM II

I was given the Hellenic tongue
my house a humble one on the sandy shores of Homer.
    My only care my tongue on the sandy shores of Homer.
There sea-bream and perch
    windbeaten verbs
green currents within the cerulean
    all that I saw blazing in my entrails
sponges, medusae
    with the first words of the Sirens
pink shells with their first dark tremors.
    My only care my tongue with its first dark tremors.
There pomegranates, quinces
    sunburnt gods, uncles and cousins
pouring oil into enormous jars;
    the exhalations rising out of ravines, scenting
osier and lentisk
    broom and pepper root
with the first chirping of the goldfinch,
    sweet psalmodies with the very first Glory to Thee.
My only care my tongue, with the very first Glory to Thee!
    There laurel and palm branches
the incense burner and the incensing
    the blessing of battles and flintlocks.
On the ground spread with the vineyard cloth
    fumes of roasting meat, the cracking of eggs
and Christ is Risen
    with the first gunfiring of the Greeks.
Secret loves with the first words of the Hymn.
    My only care my tongue, with the first words of the Hymn!

ODE 5

With the lamp of the star   *   I went out to the skies
In the meadow's chill mist   *   on the earth's only shore
Where I might find my soul   *   that four-leaf teardrop!

Myrtles in their sorrow   *   silvered over with sleep
Have now bedewed my face   *   I blow hard, plod alone
Where I might find my soul   *   that four-leaf teardrop!

O guide of all light rays   *   Magician of bedrooms
Soothsayer who knows what   *   the future brings, tell me
Where I might find my soul   *   that four-leaf teardrop!

My girls are in mourning   *   for century on century
My young men bear weapons   *   but not one of them knows
Where I might find my soul   *   that four-leaf teardrop!

Nights with a hundred arms   *   in the vast firmament
Set my entrails astir   *   This agony burns me
Where I might find my soul   *   that four-leaf teardrop!

With the lamp of the star   *   I went out to the skies
In the meadow's chill air   *   on the earth's only shore
Where I might find my soul   *   that four-leaf teardrop!

ODE 7

This oh this world * is the same world
Of many suns and dustclouds * of uproars and vespers
The weaver of constellations * the silverer of seamoss
In memory's waning * in the dreamworld's aurora
This same world * this world is
A cymbal a cymbal * and distant futile laughter!

This oh this world * is the same world
The plunderer of pleasures * the ravager of fountains
High above Cataclysms * far below all Hurricanes
The crooked, the hump-backed * the hairy, the sanguine
Piping at nighttime * fluting in daytime
This platycephalic * this macrocephalic
On the macadam of towns * on the jib-sails of prairies
The involuntary * and the voluntary
King Solomon * and Haggith's son.

This oh this world * is the same world
Of ebb tides and orgasms * of remorse and stormclouds
The inventor of zodiacs * the daredevil of skydomes
At the ecliptic's edge * to the Creation's far end
This same world * this world is
A trumpet a trumpet * and a distant futile cloud!

ODE 11

I shall be tonsured as a monk   *   of all verdant things
And modestly shall I serve   *   the order of all birds
To the matin of each Fig Tree   *   I shall come from nights
Dewdrenched   *   bringing in my lap
Cerulean   *   rose and violet
And I shall light up   *   all the valiant
Waterdrops   *   I, more valiant than all.

For my icons I shall leave im   *   maculate maidens
Dressed in the linen only   *   of the wide-spreading sea
I shall pray that my purity   *   take on the myrtle's
Instinct   *   the muscles of beasts
That in my vig   *   orous entrails I
May choke the vapid   *   the vile the perverse
Forever   *   I, more vigorous than all.

There shall come and go times of trans   *   gression of all kinds
Of profiting of pricing   *   of flogging of remorse
Then the Bucephalos of blood   *   will charge enraged to
Lash out   *   on my white yearnings
Manliness and   *   love and light. Then snif-
Ing them out to be   *   the more powerful
He whinnied   *   I, more powerful than all.

But when the sixth hour of all the   *   erect lilies strikes
At that hour when my judgment   *   shall make a breach in Time
Then the eleventh commandment   *   will leap from my eyes:
This world   *   will or will not be
Birth pangs the Aye   *   Deification
Which I in my soul's   *   justice will have pro-
Claimed to all   *   I, the most just man of all.

VI PROPHETIC

Many years after the Sin they called Arete in the churches and blessed. Holy relics of old stars and cobwebbed corners of the sky swept by the storm to be born out of the mind of man. And Creation, paying now for the works of ancient Governors, shall shudder with horror. Confusion shall fall upon Hades and its planking will give way under the great pressure of the sun, which at first will hold back its rays, sign that the time has come for dreams to be avenged. And afterward it will speak, to say: Exiled Poet, tell me, what do you see in your century?

—I see nations, once arrogant, given over to the wasp and the sour grass.

—I see axes in the air splitting busts of Emperors and Generals.

—I see a merchant stooping to collect profit from his own dead body.

—I see a sequence of meanings, secret and shoddy.

Many years after the Sin they called Arete in the churches and blessed. But before this, lo, many handsome Philips and many Roberts will be created to fall in love with themselves at the triple crossroads. They will wear their rings backward, they will comb their hair with a nail, they will adorn their chests with skulls to allure the prostitutes. And the prostitutes will be astounded and they will consent. In order that the saying may come true: that near is that day when beauty shall be surrendered to the flies of the Market Place. And the body of the whore will rage with indignation, not having anything else to crave. And the whore will become the accuser of wise men and mighty, bringing as witness on her behalf the seed she had served so faithfully. And she will cast off curses from upon her, stretching out her hand toward the East and shouting: Exiled Poet, speak, what do you see in your century?

—I see the colors of Hymettos at the sacred foundation of our New Civil Code.

—I see young Myrtó, the whore from Síkinos, raised as a stone statue in the square of the Market Place with its Fountains and its Sitting Lions.

—I see young men, I see girls in the annual Drawing by Lot of Couples vying.

—And high in the ether I see the Erechtheum of Birds flying.

Holy relics of old stars and cobwebbed corners of the sky swept by the storm to be born out of the mind of man. But before this, lo, generations will guide their ploughs over the barren earth. And the Governors will secretly count their human merchandise, declaring wars. Whereupon the Policeman and the Military Judge will be sated, leaving gold to the insignificant that they may themselves collect the wages of insult and martyrdom. And large ships will hoist flags, martial music will take to the streets, balconies will shower the Victor with flowers—who shall be living in the stench of corpses. And next to him, unfolding to his measure, darkness will gape open like a pit, crying: Exiled Poet, speak, what do you see in your century?
—I see Military Judges burning like candles on the great table of the Resurrection.
—I see Policemen offering their blood as sacrifice to the purity of the skies.
—I see the unending revolution of plants and flowers.
—I see the gunboats of Love's powers.

And Creation, paying for the works of the ancient Governors, will shudder with horror. Confusion shall fall upon Hades, and the planking will give way under the great pressure of the sun. But before this, lo, young men will sigh, and their blood for no reason at all will grow old. Shorn convicts will beat their platters on their iron bars. All factories will fall empty, but after the requisition they will be filled again to produce dreams conserved in myriads of tin cans and in a thousand varieties of bottled nature. And lean years will come and pale, wrapped in bandages. And each man will have his few grams of happiness. And all things within him already will have turned to beautiful ruins. Then, having no other exile to lament, and emptying the storm's health out of his open chest, the Poet will return to stand amid the beautiful ruins. And the first words this last of men shall say will be for the grass to grow tall and for women to emerge at his side like a sunray. And once more he will worship woman and lay her on the grass, as commanded. And dreams will be avenged, and together they will sow generations unto the ages of ages!

111

PSALM XVII

Now I'm marching on to a distant and sinless land.
Now imponderable beings follow me
    with polar iridescence in their hair
with a pure golden glaze over their skin.
    I cut through grasses with my knee for prow
and my breath blows away from the earth's face
    the last cloud-fluffs of sleep.
Trees march by my side, against the wind.
    I gaze on mysteries great and paradoxical:
Helen's crypt is a fountain.
    The shape of the cross a trident entwined with dolphins.
Unholy barbed wire a white portal
    through which I shall pass in glory.
The words that betrayed me the slaps I've endured
    have turned into myrtles and palms:
pealing out hosannas for my coming!
    I see scarcity as sensuous fruit,
slanting olive trees with azure between their fingers
    like years of fury behind prison bars.
And an endless shore, wet with the enchantment of lovely eyes:
    the sea-depths of Marína.
Where I shall walk in purity.
    The tears that betrayed me and the humiliations endured
have turned into breezes and hovering birds:
    pealing out hosannas for my coming!
Now I'm marching on to a distant and sinless land.

PSALM XVIII

Now I'm marching on to a distant and unwrinkled land.
Now azure girls follow me
    and stone ponies
with the sun's wheel on their wide brows.
    Generations of myrtles recognize me
from the time I trembled on the iconostasis of water,
    crying out to me, holy, holy.
He that defeated Hell, he that liberated Love
    he is the Prince of Lilies.
And for a moment I was once more painted
    by those same zephyrs of Crete,
that crocus yellow might receive justice from the empyrean.
    Now in whitewash I enclose and entrust
my true Laws.
    Blessed, I say, are the strong who decode the Immaculate,
for their teeth alone is the grape-nipple that intoxicates
    on the breasts of volcanoes and the vineshoots of virgins.
Behold, let them follow in my footsteps!
    Now I'm marching on to a distant and unwrinkled land.
Now it is the hand of Death
    that bestows Life,
and sleep does not exist.
    The churchbells of midday are ringing
and slowly on sunhot rocks are engraved these words:
    NOW and AYE and WORTHY IT IS
Aye aye and now now warble the birds.
    WORTHY is the price paid.

from GLORIA

WORTHY the mountain pass that opens
through clouds an endless azure pathway
    a voice that went astray in the valley
an echo the day drank up like balsam

    The effort and strain of oxen hauling
a heavy grove of olive trees westward
    the unruffled smoke that is always striving
to disperse the works man has created

    WORTHY the path where the oil lamp passes
filled now with ruins and black shadows
    the page that under the earth was written
the song the Slender Girl sang in Hades

    The wood-carved beasts on the iconostasis
and the fish-flashing the ancient poplars
    those girls with stone arms, the enchanting Korai
and Helen's neck like a long shoreline

    THE STAR-STUDDED trees with their good graces
the musical notation of another cosmos
    the ancient belief there exists forever
what is very close by and yet invisible

    The shadow that leans them on their sides earthwards
some nuance of yellow in their remembrance
    their ancient dancing above the gravestones
and far beyond all price their wisdom

               The Olive, the Pomegranate, the Peach
             the Pine, the Poplar, the Plane
              the Oak, the Beach, the Cypress

    WORTHY most worthy the causeless teardrop
that slowly dawns in the lovely glances
    of children who hand in hand go walking
of children who gaze at each other unspeaking

The lovers stammering on rock formations
a lighthouse discharging the sorrow of centuries
　　the cricket insistent as stings of conscience
and the woolen sweater left to the hoarfrost

　　The perjuring mint so acrid when bitten
two lips that cannot consent—however
　　the "goodbye" that gleams for a while on lashes
and then the world grown dim forever

　　The heavy and slow church organ of hurricanes
Herakleitos's voice destroyed of its utterance
　　the other the invisible side of murderers
and the small "why" that remains unanswerable

　　WORTHY most worthy the hand returning
from a heinous murder and is now enlightened
　　of what in truth is this world that surpasses
what is the "now" and the "aye" of the cosmos:

　　NOW to the wild beast of the myrtle *Now* to the cry of May
AYE to full consciousness and *Aye* to the full moon's ray

　　Now now to hallucination and the mimicry of sleep
Aye aye to the word itself and *Aye* to the astral's Keel

　　Now to the lepidoptera's swift undulating cloud
Aye to the lofty hovering light the Mysteries enshroud

　　Now to the husk of Earth and *now* to Dominance
Aye to the Soul's sustenance and *aye* to all quintessence

　　Now to the still incurable melanosis of the moon
Aye to the Galaxy's gold-glittering azure sheen

　　Now to the amalgam of peoples and the Black Number
Aye to the statue of Justice and the Great Staring Eye

　　Now to the humiliation of the gods *Now* to the ashes of Man
Now now to Nothingness
　　　　　　　　　　and *Aye* to the small world, the Great!

115

SIX AND ONE REMORSES FOR THE SKY

BEAUTY AND THE ILLITERATE

Often, in the Dormition of Twilight, her soul from across the
     mountains would take on a certain lightness, though the day
     were harsh and the morrow unknown.

But when the shades of night were deepening, and a priest's hand
     would rise above the small garden of the dead, She

Alone, erect, with those few domestic familiars of the night—the
     rosemary blowing and the sooty smoke of kilns—kept vigil
     at the threshold of the sea,

Strangely beautiful!

Words barely those of waves or half-guessed in a rustling, and
     others that resemble those of the dead, and that are startled
     amid the cypress trees, like strange signs of the zodiac whirled
     round and illuminated her magnetic head. And an

Unbelievable clarity permitted the true landscape to appear at a
     great distance within her

Where, close by the river, lowering men fought the Angel, show-
     ing in what manner Beauty is born

Or that which we otherwise call a tear.

And as long as her meditation endured, you felt it overbrimmed
     her countenance, which glowed with bitterness at the eyes,
     and with her enormous cheekbones, like those of an ancient
     Temple Prostitute

Stretched between the furthest tips of Canis Major and Virgo.

"Far from the pestilence of the city, I dreamt of being at her side
     in a wilderness where a tear has no meaning, and where the
     only light comes from a conflagration that consumes all my
     possessions.

"Shoulder to shoulder, we both bore together the weight of what
     shall come to be, sworn to utter quietude and the joint
     sovereignty of the stars,

119

"As though I did not understand, I the illiterate one, that it is exactly there, in utter quietude, where the most execrable noises are heard,

"And how, from the moment loneliness became unbearable in the heart of man, it has scattered and sown stars!"

THE AUTOPSY

Well, it was found that the gold of the olive root had dripped into the leaves of his heart.

And because of the many times he had kept vigil close by a candlestick, waiting for dawn to break, a strange ardor had gripped him to the marrow.

A little below the skin, the cerulean line of the horizon in a hue intense, and ample traces of azure in the blood.

It seems that the cries of birds, which in hours of great loneliness he had learned by heart, had all burst out together, so that it had not been possible for the knife to penetrate to any great depth.

Probably the intention sufficed for the Evil

Which he confronted—it is evident—in the terrifying posture of the innocent. His eyes open and proud, the whole forest still moving on his unblemished retina.

In his brain nothing but a shattered echo of the sky.

And only in the conch of his left ear, a few grains of delicate, extremely fine sand, as in seashells. Which indicates that many times he had plodded by the sea, utterly alone, with the withering grief of love and the roar of the wind.

And as for those flakes of fire on his groin, they showed that in truth he had moved time many hours ahead whenever he had merged with a woman.

We shall have early fruit this year.

SLEEP OF THE VALIANT

They still smell of frankincense, and their features are scorched from their passage through the Vast Dark Places.

There where the Immovable suddenly hurled them

Prone, on a land where even its smallest anemone were enough to embitter the air of Hell

(One hand outstretched, as though it were striving to grasp the future, the other under the desolate head turned sideways,

As though it were seeing for the last time, deep in the eyes of a disemboweled horse, the heaped ruins smoking).

There Time released them. One wing, the most red, covered the world, while the other was already tenderly moving in the distance,

And not a single wrinkle or pang of remorse, but at a great depth

The ancient immemorial blood beginning laboriously to dawn in the inky blackness of the sky,

A new Sun, still unripe,

Not strong enough to dissolve the hoarfrost of lambs on the living clover, yet dispelling, before a thorn could sprout, the oracle-making powers of Darkness . . .

And from the beginning, Valleys, Mountains, Trees, Rivers,

A creation of avenged emotions glowed, identical yet reversed, through which the Valiant now might pass, the Executioner slain within them,

Peasants of the infinite azure!

Neither the hour striking twelve in the bowels of the earth, nor the Polar voice falling vertically annulled their footfall.

They read the world insatiably with eyes forever open, there where the Immovable had suddenly hurled them

Prone, where vultures swooped down to savor their clay entrails and their blood.

SLEEP OF THE VALIANT *(Variation)*

They still smell of frankincense, and their features are scorched from their passage through the Vast Dark Places.

There where the Immovable suddenly hurled them

Prone, on a land where even the smallest anemone were enough to embitter the air of Hell

(One hand outstretched, as though it were striving to grasp the future, the other hand under the desolate head turned sideways,

As though it were seeing for the last time, deep in the eyes of a disemboweled horse, the heaped ruins smoldering.)

There Time released them. One wing, the most red, covered the world, while the other was already tenderly moving in the distance,

And not a single wrinkle or pang of remorse, but at a great depth

The ancient immemorial blood beginning laboriously to dawn in the inky blackness of the sky,

A new Sun, still unripe,

Not strong enough to dissolve the hoarfrost of lambs on the living clover, yet dispelling, before a thorn could sprout, the oracle-making powers of Darkness . . .

And from the beginning, Valleys, Mountains, Trees, Rivers,

A creation of avenged emotions glowed, identical yet reversed, through which the Valiant now might pass, the Executioner slain within them,

Peasants of the infinite azure!

Without months or years to turn their beards white, their eyes wandered through the seasons to restore to things their true names.

And for every infant that opened its hands, not even an echo, only the rage of innocence that continually strengthens the cataracts . . .

122

One drop of clear water, hanging courageously over the abyss, they named Arete, and gave her a lean, boyish body.

All day now young Arete descends and labors hard in those places where the earth was rotting out of ignorance, and where men inexplicably had committed their dark iniquities,

But at night she would always fly for refuge there high in the embrace of the Mountain as on a Man's hairy chest.

And the mist that ascends from the valleys, they say, is not smoke, but the nostalgia that evaporates from the crevices in the sleep of the Valiant.

LACONIC

Ardor for death so inflamed me that my radiance returned to the sun,

And it sends me back into the perfect syntax of stone and air.

Well then, he whom I sought *I am.*

O flaxen summer, prudent autumn,

Slightest winter,

Life pays the obolus of an olive leaf

And in a night of fools once again confirms with a small cricket the lawfulness of the Unhoped-For.

ORIGIN OF LANDSCAPE
or
THE END OF MERCY

All at once, the shadow of a swallow reaped the glances of those who longed for it: Noon.

Seizing a pointed pebble, the sun slowly and skillfully carved above the shoulders of the Kore of Euthydikos the small wings of zephyrs.

The light working on my flesh, there appeared on my chest for a moment a violent imprint, there where remorse had touched me, and I ran like a madman. Afterwards, amid the slanting leaves, sleep drained me dry and I remained alone. Alone.

I envied the dewdrop that glorified the lentisk shrubs unobserved. So would I like to hang in the astonished eye so fortunate as to see the end of Mercy!

Or had I been there perhaps? In the harshness of the rock, unfaulted from peak to pit, I recognized my stubborn jaws. That ripped the beast apart in another age.

And the sand in the distance, that had settled down from the delight given me by the sea once when men blasphemed and I swam hurriedly with quick strokes to abandon myself within her: was it this I was seeking, purity?

As the water reversed its current, I entered into the meaning of the myrtle shrubs where defaulting lovers hide. Once more I heard her silk brushing against my hairy chest as she panted. And the voice, "my precious" that night in the ravine where I cut the last mooring of the stars, where the nightingale watched carefully to imitate my pattern.

What anguish indeed, what derision was it not necessary for me to endure, with a little of my vow in both my eyes, my fingers beyond decay. Such must have been the years—ah yes— when I labored to make the endless azure so tender!

I spoke. And turning my face, I confronted it once more staring at me in the light. Merciless.

And this was purity.

Beautiful, pensive under the shadow of years, under the sun's semaphore, the Kore of Euthydikos brimmed with tears

As she watched me walking amid this world once more, without gods, but heavy with the burden of whatever, in living, I had snatched away from death.

All at once the shadow of the swallow reaped the glances of those who longed for it: Noon.

THE OTHER NOAH

I cast the horizons into the whitewash, and with slow but steady hand began to whiten the four walls of my future.

It is time now, I said, for lust to begin its holy career, and in a Monastery of Light keep secure that wonderful moment when the wind scraped off a bit of cloud above the farthermost tree on land.

These things which I struggled alone to find, that I might keep my bearing amid all contempt, will come—from the strong acid of the eucalyptus to a woman's rustling—to be saved in the Ark of my asceticism.

And of streams, the most distant and disregarded; and of birds the only one left me, the sparrow; and of the meager vocabulary of bitterness two, perhaps three, words: *bread, longing, love . . .*

(O Times that have warped the rainbow, and from the sparrow's beak have snatched away the crumb, and left not even the slightest murmur of clear water to spell out my love on the grass,

I, who without weeping, endured being orphaned from light, O Times, will not forgive.)

And when, gnawing at one another's entrails, man decreases, and from one generation to another

Evil rolls on and bursts into rage amidst all-devastating uranium,

125

Then the white cells of my solitude, whirling above the rust of the ruined world, will go to justify my small portion of prudence,

And, once more assembled, will open distant horizons that one by one bitter words might creak on the water's lips,

Imparting my old definition of despair

That like a bite on the leaf of a celestial eucalyptus, the holy day of sensual pleasure may emit its fragrance,

That the Lady, Bearer of Verdure, may ascend naked the stream of Time,

And who, opening her fingers with a regal deliberation, will send the bird once and forever

Over men's impious toil, where God erred, to let fall drop by drop

The trills of Paradise.

SEVEN DAYS FOR ETERNITY

SUNDAY: Morning in the Temple of the Calf Bearer. I say: May fair Myrtó become as real as a tree; and may her lamb, looking my murderer in the eyes for a moment, punish the most bitter future.

MONDAY: Presence of grass and water at my feet. Which means I exist. Before or after the glance that will turn me to stone, my right hand holding high a gigantic azure Stalk of Wheat. That I may establish the New Zodiac.

TUESDAY: Exodus of the numbers. Battle of the 1 and the 9 on a completely desolate shore, strewn with black pebbles, piles of seaweed, huge backbones of beasts on the rocks.
My two aged and beloved horses, neighing and rearing above the vapors that rise from the sea-sulphur.

WEDNESDAY: From the other side of the Thunderbolt. The charred hand that will sprout again. To smooth out the world's wrinkles.

THURSDAY: An open gate: stone stairs, heads of geraniums, and farther on transparent roofs, paper kites, fragments of pebbles in the sun. A he-goat slowly ruminates the centuries, and a smoke rises serenely between his horns.

At the very moment the gardener's daughter is being kissed secretly in the back yard, a flowerpot falls and shatters because of the great pleasure.

Ah, if I could only preserve that sound!

FRIDAY: "The Transfiguration" of women I have loved without hope. I cry out: Ma—rí—naaa! E—lé—niii! Every stroke of the bell is a spray of lilac in my arms. Then a strange light, and two dissimilar doves that pull me up high to a large house wreathed with ivy.

SATURDAY: Cypress tree of my lineage, cut down by sullen and silent men: for a betrothal or a death. They dig the earth around and sprinkle it with carnation water.

But I have already proclaimed the words that magnetize the infinite!

VILLA NATACHA

VILLA NATACHA
I

I've something to say, transparent and incomprehensible
Like warbling in a time of war.

Here in a corner where I've been sitting
To smoke my first free cigarette,
Awkward in happiness, trembling
For fear of breaking a flower or brushing a bird
And God find Himself in a difficult position because of me.
And yet all things submit to me,
The erect reeds and the tilting bell tower
And all the garden's firmament
Mirrored in my mind,
Names that resound one by one
Strangely in a strange tongue: Phlox, Aster, Cytise
Églantine, Pervenche, Colchique
Alise, Frésia, Pivoine, Myoporone
Muguet, Bleuet
Saxifrage
Iris, Clochette, Myosotis
Primevère, Aubépine, Tubéreuse
Paquerette, Ancolie, all shapes
Clearly written in the fruit: the circle, the square,
The triangle, the rhombus.
The way birds see them, that the world might become simple,
A drawing by Picasso
With a woman a child a centaur.

I say: and this will come. And the other will pass.
The world does not want much. Some slight
Thing: like an abrupt swerve of the wheel before an accident
But
Exactly
In
The opposite direction.
We've worshipped danger long enough, and it's time it
      repaid us.

131

*I dream of a revolution away from Evil and wars like that once
made away from chiaroscuro and tone by Matisse.*

II

But when two friends
Speak or fall silent—especially then—
There's no third possibility.
                              And it seems that, like friends,
Seas also communicate from afar.
A little air is enough, a bit of dark osier
Rubbed between the fingertips, and behold:
The wave? Is it this?
Is it this that speaks to you in the singular and says
"Do not forget me, do not forget me"? Is it Anaktoría?
Or perhaps not? Perhaps only the water that flows
Night and day in the small church of Saint Paraskeví?
To forget what? Who? We know nothing.

As when something of yours broke this evening,
An old friendship, a remembrance of eggshell porcelain
So that you see again now as day breaks
How unjust you were in judgment.
Your mouth bitter before you've taken your coffee—
Gesticulating without purpose you form an echo
From another life—who knows?—and it is from this
(Or, it may be, from a thought
At times so strong it protrudes)
That at once the mirror opposite you cracks from top to bottom.

I say: it's in one moment, an only moment,
Unrecognized when it does come,
That Destiny cracks,
And that he who gives, takes.

Because if not, then death
Also should be put to death and deterioration
Deteriorate and the small
Rose pebble you once
Held in your palm must also
Somewhere, millenniums away, be formed anew.

With wisdom and courage. Picasso and Laurens. All. Let's tread
on Psychology on Politics on Sociology, sunburnt, wearing a plain
white shirt.

III

Man,
Evil without wanting to be—
You might, but for a slight twist, have had a different fate.
If only you knew how to behave rightly
Even before a flower
All would be yours. Because at times from the few,
Or from only one—such is love—
We know the rest. But the crowd, see:
It stands on the edge of things
Wants everything and takes it and can keep nothing.

Already the afternoon has come
As serene as one in Mitilíni or a painting
By Theófilos while Èze and Cap-Estel extend far off,
Bays where the air disposes embraces,
Such a translucency
That you can touch the mountains and continue seeing
        that man
Who passed by hours ago
Indifferently, but now must have reached his destination.

I say, yes, these must have arrived,
War must have reached its end and the Tyrant his downfall
And fear of love before a naked woman.
They've arrived, they've arrived, it's only we who can't see,
But groping always, we fall on phantoms.

Angel, hovering in flight around here somewhere,
Invisible and much afflicted, take me by the hand.
Men have gilded the traps
And it's necessary I remain among those outside.
Because I feel that even the Unseen is present,
The only one I call Prince, when
Calmly the house

133

Anchored in the sunset
Emits unknown flashes,
And a thought, as from an assault,
Falls upon us unexpectedly as we are going elsewhere.

DEATH AND RESURRECTION OF
CONSTANDINOS PALEOLOGHOS

DEATH AND RESURRECTION OF
CONSTANDINOS PALEOLOGHOS
I

As he stood there   erect before the Gate and impregnable in his sorrow

Far from the world   where his spirit sought to bring Paradise to his measure   And harder even than stone   for no one had ever looked on him tenderly   —at times his crooked teeth whitened strangely

And as he passed by with his gaze a little beyond mankind   and from them all extracted One who smiled on him   the Real One whom death could never seize

He took care to pronounce the word *sea* clearly that all the dolphins within it might shine   And the desolation so great it might contain all of God   and every waterdrop ascending steadfastly toward the sun

As a young man he had seen gold glittering and gleaming on the shoulders of the great   And one night   he remembers   during a great storm the neck of the sea roared so it turned murky   but he would not submit to it

The world's an oppressive place to live through   yet with a little pride it's worth it.

II

Dear God what now   Who had to battle with thousands   and not only with his loneliness   Who?   He who knew with a single word how to slake the thirst of entire worlds   What?

From whom they had taken everything his   And his sandals with their criss-crossed straps and his pointed trident   and the wall he mounted every afternoon like an unruly and pitching boat   to hold the reins against the weather

And a handful of vervain   which he had rubbed on a girl's cheek
   at midnight   to kiss her   (how the waters of the moon gurgled on the stone steps three cliff-lengths above the sea . . .)

137

Noon out of night   And not one person by his side   Only his
faithful words that mingled all their colors to leave in his hand
a lance of white light

And opposite   along the whole wall's length   a host of heads
poured in plaster as far as his eyes could see

"Noon out of night—all life a radiance!"   he shouted and rushed
into the horde   dragging behind him an endless golden line

And at once he felt   the final pallor overmastering him   as it
hastened from afar.

III

Now   as the sun's wheel turned more and more swiftly   the court-
yards plunged into winter and once again emerged red from the
geraniums

And the small cool domes   like blue medusae   reached each time
higher to the silverwork the wind so delicately worked as a paint-
ing   for other times more distant

Virgin maidens   their breasts glowing a summer dawn   brought
him branches of fresh palm leaves   and those of the myrtle up-
rooted from the depths of the sea

Dripping iodine   While under his feat he heard   the prows of
black ships   sucked into the great whirlpool   the ancient and
smoked seacraft from which still erect with riveted gaze   the
Mothers of God stood rebuking

Horses overturned on dumpheaps   a rabble of buildings large and
small   debris and dust flaming in the air

And there lying prone   always with an unbroken word between
his teeth

Himself
the last of the Hellenes!

THE LIGHT TREE AND
THE FOURTEENTH BEAUTY

PALM SUNDAY

It must have been the sky of Palm Sunday because even the
birds descended with a green twig in their beaks and in my sleep

A girl paused without reason leaving her blouse unbuttoned

Glass in the light and within it kitchen tiles as far as my eye
could see a figure with fluttering veils double the house in height
with its fingers on an invisible doorknob

Rap flash air rap flash air unceasingly As afterward when some-
one becomes saintly and even new things seem old

And the children returning from the stone boat with octopi and
women from the olive presses and the donkey's bray at daybreak
above the vegetable gardens for how many years how many
centuries

"As old as the hills" my mother used to say and her hand the
arthritic one stopped like a begonia leaf

Well then Even memories run behind things to catch them in
time When old things in their turn also seem new

Legendary to those in days to come shall this day remain when no
one thought of grumbling but in a great distance in the foliage
sleek lemons glowed small suns of the ether.

THE GIRL THE NORTH WIND BROUGHT

At a great distance within the fragrance of mint I pondered where
I was going and I said that I might not be at the mercy of the
wilderness I shall find a small church to speak to

The roar of the sea ate up the darkness within me like a goat and
left me an opening that beckoned more and more to the Felicities
   But there was nothing no one

Only the divination of the wild olive tree became incandescent
around me

And all the mountain slope along the length of the sea spray and
high above my head spoke oracularly in susurration with myr-
iads of mauve quiverings and small insects like cherubim Yes yes
I agreed these seas will be avenged *One day these seas will be
avenged*

141

And then   up there   breaking away from her ruined shelter   gaining in height   and as beautiful as can be   with all the whimsies of birds in her movements   the girl the North Wind brought   appeared   and I waited

And as she proceeded a few lengths ahead   by leaning her small breasts for the wind to withstand   a terrified joy within me mounted to my eyelids and fluttered there

Ah the rages and the insanities of my country!

Kindled orbs of light burst behind her and left in the sky   something like the elusive signs of Paradise

I was in time to see for a moment   the forks between her legs grow wide   and all of the place inside   with even the little saliva of the sea   Afterwards her odor reached me   like fresh bread and wild mountain licorice

I pushed open the small wooden door and lit a candle   Because one of my ideas had become immortal.

DELOS

As   in diving   he would open his eyes underwater   to bring his skin in touch with that whiteness of memory which pursued him
   (from a certain paragraph in Plato)

Thus with the same movement he passed   straight into the heart of the sun and heard   a stone throat rising and his innocent self roaring high above the waves

And until he rose to the surface again   the coolness left him enough time to drag something incurable out of his entrails onto the seaweed and the other beautiful things under the water

In such a way that he might glow at length within the *I love* as the divine light glows in the weeping of the newly born

And this is what the sea was murmuring as legend.

THREE TIMES THE TRUTH

I

The wild bird *pit-pit* shifted truth from one rock to another   It kept nibbling *tlip-tlip* the briny water in the hollows   Some thing   Some thing   Something must *assuredly* exist

By my faith I was wracked on the wheel by waiting   I sprouted a monk's beard which I kept fondling and scratching   Some thing   Some thing   Something else must be found

Once I made up my mind   As one hauls up a boat on shore   I hauled up the man and so placed him   that I could look inside him

—Eh who is this?   —The murderer who passed   —And why such an uproar?   —The hawk the hawk is coming has come   —Very well   and who's in charge here?   —Nobody Nobody   —I didn't hear   who did he say?

But already the words had dwindled away   What now can one say   Such is truth.

II

Such is truth   When words withdraw   what can one possibly say   The sea seemed like an old farm surrounded by cypress trees

As she sat in the shallow water combing her hair   a stone woman remained petrified there with her hand high in the air   Farther on two ships were voyaging   wrapped in smoke but not advancing
    And everywhere out of springs and rosemary an *Our Father* rose like a confession   that kept ascending before it broke into dew

Our Father who art in heaven   I who have loved   I who have kept my girl like a vow   who could even catch the sun by its wings like a butterfly   *Our Father*

I lived on nothing.

III

I lived on nothing   Only words could not suffice me   As a wind
passed by   and my ears unraveled an unworldly sound   *fhiá fhioú
fhioú*   I imagined a thousand things   What fistfuls of beachstones
   What basketfuls of fresh honeybees and bulging waterjugs where
the *vvvvv* of the captive air could be heard thundering.

Some thing   Some thing   Something dæmonic but which can be
caught in the shape of an Archangel as in a net   I babbled and ran
on   I arrived and from out of language imprinted waves on my
hearing

—Eh small black promontories   I shouted   and you azure trees
what do you know of me   —*Adhói adhói adhíze*   —Eh? what?
   —*Aríio adhíize adhíse*   —I didn't hear   what did you say?
—*Adýss adýss adíze*

Until at last I felt   and let them call me crazy   that out of nothing
is born our Paradise.

ON THE REPUBLIC

Out of four stones and a little seawater   I built a Temple and sat
down to guard it

Noon bore down   and what we call thought throbbed in the globe
of a black grape ready to burst

Something must be happening in the heavens that can be caught in
the body like a wet dream

"Slowly   in the hall enlarged by its resonance   the bearded man
approached the cage and opened the small gate   so many centuries
of struggle for a slight movement like that of the railway switcher
   which all desired but no one dared

"The curtains swayed   and the sound of the bird arrived before its
image   skimming the ceiling

"It glowed around the statuary and hovered motionless above the
peristyle for a moment like a vertigo   until trees beat themselves
against the North window and you saw the radiance flicker here and
there until

"Behold her   the naked woman   with a green mist on her hair and a jacket of golden wire   came and sat gently on the tiles   with her thighs half open

"And this in my consciousness took on the meaning of a flower when danger opens within it the first tenderness   And afterwards exactly as

"In the Apocalypse   the four horses passed in a row: the black the silver   the guilty   and the dream-taken   without saddle or rider   wanting to indicate that their glory had passed away

"And that the crowd marching behind them   in a general mobilization   go to be engulfed by the Gehenna of Paradise   as it was destined

"The man opposite her parted his clothes   and his handsome animal advanced in front for a life in the land of forests and suns."

I smelled in the air the body of a fig tree   when it came to me still fresh from the pigments of the sea

As I moved above it   until   I sweetly awoke and felt its milk sticky between my thighs

I continued frenziedly to write "On the Republic" amid the extreme contritions of the infinite azure

And among large translucent leaves   For a moment the islands appeared   and still higher in the ether   all the various ways birds have of flying little by little   as far as the infinite.

LITTLE GREEN SEA

Little green sea thirteen years old
I would like to adopt you
And send you to school in Ionia
To learn of mandarins and wormwood
Little green sea thirteen years old
On the lighthouse tower at the drop of noon
To turn the sun and to hear
How fate is undone and how
From hill to hill our distant
Relatives still signal one another
Who like statues hold the air
Little green sea thirteen years old
With your white collar and your ribbon
Enter Smyrna from my window
To copy reflections for me on the ceiling
From the *God have mercy* and the *Glory be*
And with a little North Wind and a little Easterner
Turn back wave by wave
Little green sea thirteen years old
That I may sleep with you secretly
And find deep in your embrace
Broken stones: the words of God
Broken stones: fragments from Herakleitos.

THE WALL PAINTING

Having fallen in love and lived for centuries in the sea   I learned reading and writing

Until now   at a great distance behind me   I can gaze at one generation after another   the way one mountain begins

Before the other ends   And in front of me the same thing again:

The dark blue bottle   and Helen with her youthful arms   outlined against the whitewash

Pouring out wine for the Virgin   half of her body escaped already into Asia opposite

And all the embroidery   displaced in the sky   with the forked birds   the small yellow flower   and the suns.

146

THE ODYSSEY

The house amid its gardens pitched and tossed and from its large
windows you could see   the mountains opposite vanishing at times
   and at times rising high again

At the head of the stairs   with a sailor's jacket cast over his shoul-
ders   my father would begin to shout   and we all scattered right
and left   one to tie a beam firmly   another to gather up the awn-
ings quickly   before such a sudden West Wind could capsize us

No matter what   in our part of the world we always went on
voyages

Hard to windward

But carefully   as though we had known since then that bitterness
had always existed   and that Greece had never existed

Full and by

The wind swelled the midsails   *the purple waves boomed loudly
around her keel as the ship sped on*

And we coasted along the lands of the Lotos Eaters with the enduring
half-moon   islands black and bony rising out of the waters   Once
before it had been Aiolia where men wandered in their sleep accord-
ing to the weather

And as they say   twice a year   at the Equinoxes   small white
children weighing very little   fell unceasingly like soft snowflakes
   and at their first touch   melted and left a little dew

I remember a port out of the beaten track   where it was not easy to
anchor   and where the inhabitants at night glowed like fireflies

Glory be to God   we roamed everywhere   unloading oil and wine
and receiving in exchange tons of flowers   those which the natives
in their own tongue call roses   small bottles with the essence of
rare jasmine or even women

A girl suddenly   struck by the Archangel's glance   whom I took
as my slave   and even today as I write only she has stood by me

Veer to starboard

147

In the same place   as though becalmed   for the coasts were slow
to appear

"You thought you were becalmed   but the others who drew ahead
    it's they who made you appear motionless"   my father would say
    setting my thoughts straight

And I would pin his words one by one with the butterflies in my
notebook

Together with other words the wind snatched away from the basket
of the wise or the gypsy's mouth   (for years she had lived as a
bird of prey and had brought wisdom down from the mountains)

Many words without coherence as though from some torn poem
    For example   "The water the turtledove broke and my wound be-
came beautiful"   or   "Let me have nothing else but you"

And the wind continued whatever I had begun to think   and often
the sailing ships would snatch it from me   with piles of water-
melon and other fruit

In the upper room with the round porthole

Day after day the gypsy woman searched in the coffee cup   and
day after day the seven wise men of the world conversed   bent over
old charts and sextants: Thales of Miletos   Ibn Al Mansour   Sim-
eon the young Theologian   Paracelsus   Hardenburg   George the
Fisherman   and André Breton

Hard to windward

There are a thousands ways by which to learn   but to enter   thus
    into the future   naïveté is needed

You would need to know Mary the elder and Mary the younger
who place a pomegranate in bed and it is always May until morning

Somewhere along there must have been my own Near East   because

Both the Rose of Espahan and famou' Pharizad   who on one side
had golden hair and silver on the other   I had once caught in the
keyhole

Of the long narrow room which the sea tossed   now here now there
  as I tried to keep it balanced

With a longing to know   how the foot grows larger   there   where
it begins to be separated from the other   and the gleam on the knee
  or if I were lucky a glimpse of the sea urchin   for a moment   in
sea-depths unexplored

My heart beat violently   menthol water flowed over my palate   a
man by God a few days later I too then would have an opinion

Heave to

So as to make the majority understand   that power only kills   and
most important of all:

That Spring   even Spring   is a product of man

Drop anchor

I stooped within me to hear

And a warmth as from a creature in love struck me   which not
even Arabian jasmine know   that were already sprouting white as
though I had been loved

In the entwined branches and the double leaves   from which a
sickening dampness struck your nostrils   breath of stinkweed and
the piss of trees   Suddenly the other aspect

Fanned out into a mauve world   Girls Ladies   the violet and the
vienlaviéla   the sabres of Osman and the Triclinium of Nikephoros

Where only his peacock took four hours to open over the waters
  with the stitches of the watersnake here and there

Or   if rain could be sniffed in the air   it kept watch during an in-
terval of three or four days   until the sound began to fall and the
seeds

Blue and rose took fright by the thousands and trembled

But the voice of the gardener brought peace   and then all the or-
chard dropped anchor.

ARCHETYPE

The pebble's gunpowder as it exploded   brought me the island
once again and a certain shore

Where as it seems I had first seen Woman   and what it means to see
luminous rose trees at midnight   I understood all this afterwards

When I found her to be a pigeon

When I found her to be Sleep   with clusters of dew on her bosom

When I found her on a terrace being unraveled by a strong wind

Until at length only a shoulder remained and a fragment of her hair
to the right

Above the ruins and the first Evening Star.

THE LIGHT TREE
I

My mother was still living   a dark shawl thrown over her shoulders
    when it first crossed my mind to find an ending in the midst of
happiness

Death drew me like a strong light   wherein you can see nothing
else   And I did not want to know I did not want to learn what the
soul had made of the world

Sometimes   the cat that climbed on my shoulders   fixed its golden
eyes somewhere beyond me   and it was then I felt a reflection com-
ing toward me from the other side   like an incurable as they say
nostalgia

And again at other times when the piano lesson could be heard from
the parlor below   with my forehead to the windowpane I watched
above the woodpiles in the distance   a shower of white birds burst-
ing on the breakwater and turning into mist

It's not known how the wronged man and I lived together within
me   but perhaps

The wind had heard my complaint on a distant May   for see: once
or twice the Perfect appeared before my eyes   and then nothing
once more

Like a bird before its song can be caught   when it vanishes swept
away by the sun in crimson as it sets

II

Others descended as I ascended   and I heard my heels in the empty
rooms   somewhat as in a church when God is not there   Even the
vilest things are done peacefully

Someone would come   however   Perhaps even love but   At two
in the afternoon when I leaned over my window to chance on some-
thing angry or unlucky   there was only the light tree

There in the back part of the courtyard   amid the stinking weeds
and the scrap iron   however   Where no one had ever watered it
   but   I spent my days playing with my spit to sling it out from on
high   until

All at once   spring smashed the walls   the windowsill fell away
from my elbow   and I remained prone in the air gazing

At the sort of thing truth is   made all of round leaves   and a sul-
phine red on the side toward the sun   five   ten   hundreds   seized
in perpetuity by the unknown

Just like us   And even though disasters raged around us   even
though men died   even though repercussions of war arrived   sent
out again from the bowels of the Lamb   nothing touched it   For
a moment it paused to see if it could endure

Then finally advanced   implacably in the light   like Jesus Christ
and all those in love.

III

Cursed be the outside sea that had grown calm (and the house inside
had grown larger) and I was left in my bed abandoned   touched by
crosses of every kind

Of flowers and of men who from the time of the first Christmas
   had worked in Aunt Vatána's house   as all night long she flick-
ered in the empty rooms like a candle

And of Aunt Melissiní's   who had just returned from Doomsday
   and you'd say that something maroon from the Virgin still covered
her thin hair

(Sorrow   sorrow of mine that can't be spoken to   yet you are a
ship drenched in the full moon and a boundless consolation   towing
aromatic islands in my sleep with half the firmament lit   I am

Ah a man in love   and the only thing I seek ah is the only thing I do
not have)

Bits of wood drifted by and happiness scorched by the passing of the
incense burner on the hills of the nearby East   seraglios adorned
with gold and wisdom poured into a glass

I wanted the least and they punished me with more.

IV

Now in the distant island the house was no longer there   only
when the wind blew from the South would you see a Monastery in
its place   continued by the clouds to a greater height   and down
below by its subterranean foundations   the green waters splashed
and licked the walls with their heavy iron doors

I went round and round it   emitting a reddish light   from being so
much tormented and so much alone

Completely aimless monks chanted and studied   nor would anyone
open for me that I might once more see in what places I had spent
my childhood   in what places my mother had scolded me   where
the light tree had first sprouted and for the sake of whom   if it
still exists

Smoke emerged from somewhere   out of the gaze of Saint Isidore
perhaps   sending the message that

Our sufferings are as they should be   and that the present order is
not going to be overthrown

Ah where are you now my hapless light tree   where are you my
light tree   I babbled to myself and ran   it's now I need you   now
that I've even lost my name

Now when no one mourns the nightingales   and all write poems.

CYCLICAL

Courage: the sky is this
And its birds we
                              all those who do not resemble others

Submerged within us
A cereal sea with soil and huge cowsheds

The only thing left outside was the sunflower

But who is he who walks in the sun
Black   according to the sun's strength

Courage: man is this
The Canis as he is called
                              but by a hair the Canis Major

Virginal expanses   winds the nomads of June
Furrowed chestnut earth on which we clambered

Thirsty for a little luminous light as of Mount Tabor

But what is this that passes low on the ground and shudders
Like the breeze of another world arrived

Courage: death is this
On the wide poppy
                              and on the slim-slender camomile.

THE GARDEN OF THE SCORCHED HAND

However you take it   I've lost the game   here at this far edge where
the disasters of this world have placed me   I wanted to attempt a
leap swifter than disintegration

153

And as   with my head below and my feet upside down in the air   I fought to free myself of my weight   the passion that was impelling me high became so strongly inverted within me   that I found myself slanting and once again moving   in a garden flowing with white pebbles and the translucent blue of mint

With great vigor I advanced   breaking the switches of water   to see where the stars Míka and Xénia and Manió   were ascending and descending with a lit lantern in their bellies

The mastick gum of their hair stuck and   now here now there   a magnificent butterfly still only half-created   strained to disengage itself   And on the marks left by the plane tree with its wide footsteps   you could still distinguish traces from the enigma of the first man

(O youth who have suffered much   remember   that once triremes set out   crammed with wild-eyed people   Those morning reflections on bronze   the old men gesticulating and crying out   *iaí iatataí*   striking the tiles with their wooden staffs

But what flowers the tempests raised!   And what portable mountains the large nights of the Moon!   The horse that swept you off to the edge of all edges   and then afterwards the house hidden among the trees   I say   remember then the heart's weight and the beautiful head you cupped to kiss amid the white motley of jasmine

And keep in mind   keep always in mind   do you hear me?   the *ah* emitted by slaughter   the *ah* emitted by love)

Trees dripped green pits   and a golden reflection fell on gooseberries   Fruit packed in ice melted and brought strange incense down from on high   So much bliss hurt me   but I sought to live again all my destiny inverted

And as I left my thought behind like the airwake of a swallow   and as it changed colors in the water   chilly or in ringlets or translucent   I hit bottom head on   When a sun leaped up

The ether splayed out like rays   and I heard the four renowned rivers rolling down toward earth with the names of   Phison   Gihon   Tigris   Euphrates

Sun my sun my very own   Take all I have take it all   and leave me
   leave me pride   That I may not reveal a single tear   That I may
only touch you even though I burn   I shouted and spread out my
hand

The garden vanished   Spring with her strong teeth swallowed it
like an almond

And I remained upright once again   with a scorched hand   here at
the edge where disasters have placed me   to struggle with the Not
and the Impossible of this world.

WHAT CAN'T BE DONE

Oh that nostalgia might have a body so I could push it out of the
window!   That I might smash what can't be done!   Girl from
whose naked breast   God once saved me as from a life raft

And took me high above the half-moon over the walls   that out of
my indiscretions

You might not be exposed   and the Fates mark you down   As
indeed it came to be   Because such are the things life loves and
wants   though we believe them to be elsewhere

And from the other side of love   and from the other side of death
   we walk in our sleep until   that which has become flesh of our
flesh   unbearably constricted now   flares up within us in fire like
phosphorus   and we awaken

Time   yes   proceeds in a straight line   but love goes vertically
   and either they are cut in two   or never meet   But that which re-
mains like

Sand in rooms from a strong wind   and the spider   and outside on
the threshold

The wailing wolf with its round eye   all these seem possible   the
mountains of Crete above all   that in snow were mine as a boy and
I found them again in their coolness   But what does it matter

If at times you are free and at times a victor   for the sun again will
set and remain all around you

With a quietness full of ruined shores   where still the clouds descend to eat grass   a little before it becomes dark forever

As though men had come to an end   and nothing of any importance remained to be said.

THE MONOGRAM

I shall mourn always—do you hear me?—for you alone in Paradise.

THE MONOGRAM
I
Like a switchman at the rails it shall be Fate's intent
To shunt the lines of our palm elsewhere
And time for a moment will consent

How else, since men do love each other?

Our feelings then shall be acted out by the sky
And innocence shall smite the world
With the sharpness of dark death when *I*

II
Shall mourn the sun and mourn all future years
And we not here, and I shall sing of other things that disappear
If these are true

Bodies in concord and boats that sweetly collide
Guitars under the water that flutter and flick
The "Believe me" and the "Don't"
Once in the air and once again in music

And our hands, these two small beasts that wait
Then seek to mount each other secretly
Basil in flowerpots by the open courtyard gate
And fragments of the sea that follow us as we climb
Beyond the hedge and over the dry stone wall
The windflower that comes and perches on our hand as all
Its mauve quivers thrice in three days over the waterfall

If these are true I sing
Of the woven country coth and the wooden beam
Of the Gorgon on the wall with her flowing hair
And the cat that out of the darkness watched us there

Boy with your frankincense and your crimson cross
When night darkens over the rocks far out of reach, I lament the
   time
When I touched a garment and all the world was mine.

III
This is how I speak of you and of me

Because I love you and being in love I know how to enter
Like the full moon from everywhere and find your small feet
Under the vast bedsheet
And how to pluck the petals of the jasmine flower—for I have the
    power
To come when you are sleeping and blow and snatch you away
To moondrenched passageways and secret arcades of the sea
To mesmerized trees with cobwebs shining silverly
The waves have heard
How well you caress and how well you kiss
How you say the "what" and the "eh" in whispers
Around the neck of the bay in its overflow
We are *always* the light and the shadow

Always the small star you and I the dark ship at night
Always the small harbor you and I the lantern placed to the right
The wet splashwall and the glittering of oars
High up in the house with its bowers of marigold
The bound rose bushes and the water growing cold
Always the stone statue you and *always* I its lengthening shadow
The leaning window shutter you and I the wind that opens it on
    the meadow
Because I love you and in loving you divert
The coin that is *always* you for I am the adoration that converts:

So much for the night and so much for the wind's outcry
So much for the waterdrop in the air so much for stillness
And around us the despotic sea seething
The arcade of the starry sky
So much for your slightest breathing

That now I have nothing more
Amid the four walls the ceiling the floor
To shout at because of you as my own voice smites me
To smell of you while men shrink with fright
Because mankind cannot bear whatever is untried
Or brought in from elsewhere and it's early do you hear me
It's still too early in this world my love

To speak of you and of me.

IV

It's still too early in this world *do you hear me*
The monsters have not as yet been tamed *do you hear me*
My lost blood and the pointed knife
Do you hear me
Running in the heavens like a ram
And breaking the branches of the stars *do you hear me*
It is I *do you hear me*
I love you *do you hear me*
I hold you and lead you and dress you
In Ophelia's white bridal gown *do you hear me*
Where are you leaving me and where are you going and who *do*
        you hear me

Is holding your hand above the cataclysm

That day will come *do you hear me*
When volcano lava and huge tropical vines
Will bury us and thousands of years afterwards *do you hear me*
Will turn us into dazzling fossils *do you hear me*
That man's hardness of heart *do you hear me*
May glitter above them
And cast us away in a thousand pieces *do you hear me*

In the waters *do you hear me*
I count my pebbles one by one *do you hear me*
And time is a huge church *do you hear me*
Where the eyes of Saints from time to time
Do you hear me
Flow with real tears *do you hear me*
And bells high up in the air *do you hear me*
Open up deep passageways through which I may pass
Where angels await me with candles and funeral hymns
I won't go anywhere *do you hear me*
Either no one alone or both of us together *do you hear me*

This flower of the thunderstorm *do you hear me*
And of love
We have plucked once and forever *do you hear me*
And it can never blossom in any other way *do you hear me*
In any other earth on any other star *do you hear me*
That soul does not exist that air does not exist
That we have ourselves once touched *do you hear me*

And no gardener was ever so lucky in times past *do you hear me*

After so many winters and so many harsh winds *do you hear me*
As to make one flower sprout but only we *do you hear me*
In the middle of the sea
Out of love's longing alone *do you hear me*
Have we raised an entire island *do you hear me*
With caverns and coves and flowering cliffs
Listen—listen
Who is talking to the waters who is weeping—*do you hear*
Who is trying to find the other who is shouting—*do you hear*
It's I who is talking, it's I who is weeping *do you hear me*
I love you I love you *do you hear me.*

V

For you and about you have I spoken in ancient times
With veteran old rebels and grannies grown wise
Of where you once acquired that sadness of a wild animal
That reflection on your face as of water quivering
Of why I find myself impelled to nestle by your side at all
I who have never wanted love but only the wind's wing
Only the bareback rearing sea's wild galloping

But no one had heard of you
Neither the dittany nor the mushroom
Nothing in the upland reaches of Crete
For you only did a god consent to guide my shaping hand

At times here and at times there in every round and pleat
Of the shore of the face, round the bay and the hair
As it fluttered to the left in the hill's high air

Your body in the pose of the solitary pine tree's commitment
Eyes of pride and the translucent
Depth in the house with its old sideboard
Its yellow laces and its cypress wood
Alone, waiting to see where you would first appear
High up on the roof terrace or far back in the courtyard section
With the horse of Saint George and the egg of the Resurrection

As though out of a ravaged mural's tableau
As large as small life wanted you to be
You came to fit into the candle's flame the volcano's stentorian glow

You of whom no one had ever heard or seen
Nothing in the wilderness or the crumbled houses
Neither the ancestors buried at the far end by the courtyard curb
Nor the old sorceress with her magic herb

Only I have known of you perhaps or that music
I cast out of me though it returns with a stronger accent
Of you only the unformed breast of a twelve-year-old as later
It turns toward the future with its crimson crater
Of you only the bitter fragrance that like a pin
Pierces into the body and pricks the memory's discipline
For it is here our soil our pigeons and our ancient earth have
    always been.

VI

Much have I seen, and in my mind the earth seems more beautiful
More beautiful the sharp stone
Amid golden mists more beautiful
The dark blue waters of the isthmus and roofs over the waves
    rising tall
More beautiful than sunrays through which with untouching feet
    you pace
Invisible over the sea mountains like the goddess of Samothrace

So much have I looked upon you that now for me it's enough
For all time to be judged as innocent my love
There in the wake your passing leaves behind
Which like an untried dolphin my soul must seek and find

To follow after, playing with its white and blue

163

Victory, victory by which I have been conquered too
Before love came and now together with our love
Follow the passion flower and the mimosa tree
Go, follow after, go although I'm lost eternally

I'm *alone* though the sun you hold is a newborn infant
I'm *alone* though I am the father who must lament
And may an oleander leaf become the proffered word I send
The strong wind is *alone* and *alone* the thoroughly round
Pebble that winks now in the dark depths profound
The fisherboy who nets his Paradise then casts it back into the
    centuries.

VII

I have mapped out an island *in Paradise*
That looks like you and a house by the seaside

With a large bed and a small door
I have cast a sound into the bottomless depths of the sea
To look at myself each morning when I arise

And see the half of you passing over the watery floor
As I weep for your other half *in Paradise*.

THE SOVEREIGN SUN

NARRATOR
THE SUN
WINDS
GIRL
CHORUS OF MEN
CHORUS OF WOMEN
SINGERS

THE SOVEREIGN SUN

NARRATOR

The Sun the Sun the Sovereign Sun
    of all stone-players the champion

Beyond the world's far edge and brink
    on Tenedos must set and sink

His chin is made of flames and fire
    his forks are made of golden wire.

THE SUN

O come you shores and come you seas
    vineyards and golden olive trees

out of my noonday's interim
    come listen to my bulletin

"No matter what lands I roam and love
    this is the land I'm enamored of."

From the far middle of every steep
    to the far middle of every deep

spread crimson yellow fields of grain
    the emerald and boundless main

"No matter what lands I roam and love
    this is the land I'm enamored of,"

with its small gamins demoniac
    riding astride a dolphin's back

with its young girls on every strand
    burning stark naked on the sand

with all its daffy roosteroos
    and all its cock-a-doodle-doos!

CHORUS OF WOMEN

Because we have no bread my friend
such things are hard to understand

they've fought us so for years on end
we've not had time to breathe or mend.

A WOMAN

The birds have gone and flown elsewhere
yet I on this wave-pounded shore

have tried to build my house and home.
It won't stand up on sand and foam.

ALL TOGETHER

What in four months we built with joy
we must in eight long months destroy

and every full-grown olive tree
costs an entire family.

A WOMAN

What lovely secret dreams I made
of all the children I would raise

who would have thought who would have said
they'd all be sent to be killed instead.

ALL TOGETHER

Some went to fight on ships at sea
some went to fight on mountains free

each with his khaki shirt but oh
my curses on both friend and foe!

NARRATOR

The sun heard and was horrified
then cast his crimson rays of light

as burst in flames the mountain woods
and all the upland neighborhoods.

THE SUN

Hey what's all this audacity
come all my winds from land and sea

North South East West, all my ménage
come quickly make your reportage.

FIRST WIND

I push ships if I want to, I halt them if I like
I split two mountains apart, then plunge on a long hike

I enter into love affairs, but soon grow harassed
and when I'm told their secrets, then I grow embarrassed

I send out news to all, to everyone confess
the mind of man wears out, and then alack alas.

SECOND WIND

Cursed be that bitter hour, he who here has might
blesses what's wrong side up, and then will call it right.

You never hear him mention what's the weak man's due
but turns day into night, and then will swear it's true.

Wherever there's a large door, you'll find him back of it
then find that he's vamoosed, whenever you open it.

THIRD WIND

Wheat fields of Saloníki and mountains of Moriás
where are your captured castles, where are your villages?

Look at the waning half-moon now sailing through the air
look at the lovely girl, may I take joy of her!

On Monday she grows tall, on Tuesday goes to war
on Wednesday bends her knee, on Thursday is no more.

FOURTH WIND

O roads well worn and trodden, O roads not worn at all
*   who has traversed their length, who has not passed at all?*

But those who took these roads and waded deep in blood
*   not God or man can stop them in their fortitude.*

Poor miserable creations, you've been filled with lies
*   all the world's crazy fools have now been mobilized!*

NARRATOR

Full of suspicion and complaint
*   the world turns thrice in its constraint*

midnight evening and noontide
*   all the rooms are opened wide*

on threshing floor and farmyard gate
*   clairvoyant spirits watch and wait*

on glowing embers of a star
*   they bring and burn their streaming hair*

then stop the smallest angel stum-
*   bling by to play their fie-fo-fum.*

My dear you've grown too grim and grey
*   yet you've not withered the world away*

they say that both your black and white
*   are blown by every wind in sight*

and a small girl but nine years done
*   sings for the sake of everyone.*

GIRL

Two for you and three for me
*   a game of five green stones you see*

I enter through the garden trellis
*   and how's your health Miss Amaryllis?*

Waterpools and fountain streams
*   and all my dissipated dreams!*

O cricket mine now go crick-crick
    and spin the spinning spindle quick

if to the right I hop with glee
    I'll bump the pomegranate tree

if to the left I hop and carry
    I'll fall in bushes of raspberry

in my one hand I grasp to see
    an enormous bumblebee

and in my other hand hold high
    a large biting butterfly.

CHORUS

A pebble cast in clearest water
    is this girl's longing so long sought for

circles opening ring on ring
    then all your form encompassing

the mountain's a flowerpot held high
    with gold geraniums of the sky

Sun O Sun O thrice my Sun
    send me a word, if only one.

WINDS

Now come and hear us also, who have just returned
    of islands and of cities we have known and learned

of Crete and Mitilíni, Sámos and Ikariá
    Náxos and Santoríni, Rhodes and Kérkira

of houses large and whitewashed, houses that hum and drone
    perched high above the waters, perched on deep dark stone

Xánthi, Thessaloníki, Vérria, Kastoriá
    Yánnina, Mesolóngi, Spárta and Mistrá

of belfries and of rooftops in the cloudy skies
    that both compose a sorrow and a Paradise.

THE SUN

I've never seen so strange or beautiful a land
as this that fate has chanced to make my fatherland.

He casts a net for fishes, sets up ships on turf
then catches birds on wing, plants gardens on the surf

kisses the ground and weeps, then sails to lands afar
remains at all five crossroads, and grows to manhood there

takes up a stone at random, then drops and lets it be
but when he cuts and carves it, what wonders form and flee

sets foot on a small dinghy, and sails far out at sea
goes searching for rebellions, hungers for tyranny

gives birth to five great men, but beats them black and blue
and then heigh-ho, good riddance, he glorifies the crew.

CHORUS OF MEN

There's nothing much a man may want
but to be quiet and innocent

a little food a little wine
at Christmas and at Easter time

wherever he may build his nest
may no one there disturb his rest.

But everything has all gone wrong
they wake him up at break of dawn

then come and drag him to and fro
eat up what little he has and lo

from out his mouth from out of sight
and in a moment of great delight

they snatch his morsel in an evil hour.
Hip hip hurrah for those in Power!

CHORUS OF WOMEN

Hip hip hurrah for those in Power
for them there is no "I" or "our."

172

Hip hip hurrah for those in Power
   whatever they see they must devour.

NARRATOR

The Sun the Sun the Sovereign Sun
   of all stone-players the champion

has only to open his mouth a bit
   for a spring fragrance benefit

then every bird bursts out in song
   and bovine beasts moo all day long

and all the winds to all their heights
   are filled with many-colored kites.

THE SUN

What can I say to you women, and what can't I say
   of truth and consolation, nor yet be ashamed to say?

I've only at times to hear you to grow sad and bowed
   and then I take to darkness or hide behind a cloud

but then at times by God I preen and strut with pride
   put on my crimson garments then march out and ride

down to the very earth where roots participate
   where flowers turn toward me and with me fecundate

till medicines that cure us and all loveliness
   form firmest ties with poisons in all secretness.

The light I carry with me, and love itself I fear
   for both of these even I, the sun, must pay most dear

all the world's dirty linen, all its sludge and slime
   time casts them all within me to the end of time

and as I hang on high above the water's wash
   and as I travel far through darkest Tartarus

173

all tyrannies tormentors killers and murderers
  I put them to the grindstone for our future years

I grind them and I churn them and on earth alight
  that gave us this grim darkness, to drink them up as light.

Take courage O my pigeons my anemonies
  my beauties my companions and my love-e-lies

wherever dark and gloom is woven and spun all day
  turn into small small suns, my dears, and grind away

evil itself does bring to birth the blessèd day
  and every narrow lane must lead to the broad highway

and there exactly in both dark and ruination
  memory sinks deep roots in fragrant exhalation.

Root O bitter rootstem and my secret spring
  now give us of your pride and take away our sting

by all the windows of every room in every house
  strawberry trees and laurel leaves and palm tree boughs

their sleeves rolled up around a table with red wine
  youngsters and oldsters and grown men sit down and dine.

Take up a flaming mood, take up your mandolin
  take up your golden speech, take up your tambourine

and let the song begin, and let nostalgia rise
  till mind and thought both give and take of Paradise.

What with the "get" and with the "ful" and with the "ness"
  the whole world's wrongs now fall into for-get-ful-ness.

THE CRAZY BOAT

A boat adorned and decked sails out for mountains oh
  and there begins maneuvers with heave-to, heave-ho

weighs anchor by a pine tree grove and takes aboard
  a cargo of fresh mountain air at lee and port.

174

She's made of blackest stone, she's made of flimsy dream
*   her boatswain is naïve, her sailors plot and scheme*

she's come from the deep depths of ancient bygone times
*   and here unloads her troubles and her trembling sighs.*

O come my Lord and Jesus, I speak and am struck daft
*   on such a loony vessel on such a crazy craft*

we've sailed for years on end, and still we've kept afloat
*   we've changed a thousand skippers on this balmy boat*

we never paid the slightest heed to cataclysms
*   but plunged headlong in everything with optimisms*

and high up on our lookout mast we keep for sentry one
*   who ever and anon remains our Sun our Sovereign Sun!*

NOTES

NOTES

NOTES

INTRODUCTION, p. 3.

Kóstas Ouránis and Kóstas Kariotákis, p. 4: Poems, biographies, bibliographies, and/or analyses of all modern Greek poets mentioned in this Introduction can be found in *Modern Greek Poetry: From Caváfis to Elýtis*, translated and with Introduction, Notes and essay "On Translation" by Kimon Friar (Simon & Schuster, 1973).

grapehard girls, p. 9: From "Yellow," in *Sun the First*.

countryside of the open heart, p. 10: From "Birth of Day," in *Orientations*.

extensions . . . body, p. 10: Andréas Karandónis.

With what Stones what Blood what Iron, p. 15: In *Sun the First*.

Proud Night, p. 15: In *Orientations*.

Depth, p. 15: In *Orientations*.

death is . . . leaves unused, p. 18: In a radio interview, taped in Rome and Paris, May–June 1951.

the thought . . . lasting pain, p. 22: *Paradise Lost*, bk. 1, 54–56.

hurled headlong . . . perdition, p. 22: Ibid., bk. 1, 45–47.

adamantine chains and penal fire, p. 22: Ibid., bk. 1, 48.

General Yánnis Makriyánnis, p. 27: See "Makriyánnis," in *On the Greek Style*, by George Seféris, translated by Rex Warner and T. D. Frangópoulos (Little, Brown, 1966).

Byzantine troparia . . . Erotókritos, p. 29: For discussion and examples, see *The Penguin Book of Greek Verse*, by Constantine Trypanis (Penguin Books, 1971).

Papadhiamándis, p. 29: For this literary figure and others mentioned in this Introduction, see *A History of Modern Greek Literature*, by C. Th. Dimarás, translated by Mary P. Gianos (State University of New York Press, 1972).

katharévousa, p. 29: For a discussion of the language question, see "Introduction" to Friar's *Modern Greek Poetry*. For more extensive expositions, see *Kazantzákis and the Linguistic Revolution in Greek Literature,* by Peter Bien (Princeton University Press, 1972); also *Studies in the Greek Language,* by Basil G. Mandilarás (Athens, 1972).

Molotov cocktails . . . fall silent, p. 35: Interviewed by Yórghos Pilihós in the newspaper *Ta Néa,* January 27, 1973.

All forms . . . into tears, p. 36: Ibid.

ORIENTATIONS, p. 45. *Départ . . . neufs:* "Departure in new affection and new noise," from "Départ," in *Illuminations* by Arthur Rimbaud.

OF THE AEGEAN, p. 47: This is the first of three parts.

THE GIRLS WHO TROD ON THE FEW, BREASTING THE CURRENT, and ADO-LESCENCE OF DAY, pp. 47, 48: Parts V, X, and XV of "Pellucid Skies" in twenty-one parts.

IN THE SERVICE OF SUMMER

ANNIVERSARY, p. 61

. . . even the weariest river . . . sea: from "The Garden of Proserpine," in *Poems and Ballads: First Series* by Algernon Charles Swinburne.

ODE TO SANTORÍNI, p. 64. Santoríni, the ancient Thera, is one of the Cycladic Islands in the Aegean, composed primarily of volcanic rock, pumice stone, and china clay. According to recent archeological theory, it was the site of Atlantis.

AGE OF BLUE MEMORY, p. 67

The Lord Will Provide: Greek boats are often named after saints or biblical phrases such as these.

immortal water: A legend dating from antiquity relates that if anyone bathed in or drank from the waters of the Styx on Mount Hélmos near Patras, he would become immortal. This phrase often occurs in Greek folk songs and legends.

MELANCHOLY OF THE AEGEAN, p. 68

Madonna: See first note to "Age of Blue Memory," above.

muted water: Literally, "speechless water." On June 24, John the Baptist's birthday, a boy or girl fetches water in a jug from a well or fountain. The one carrying the water must not talk to anyone on the way. It is taken to a house where each of the congregated boys and girls of the village throws some personal belonging into the jug: a ring, an earring, an apple. The jug is then covered with a red cloth and exposed to the stars all night. In the morning, as the articles are taken out one by one, divinatory, satirical, or laudatory couplets about the owners are recited, often predicting whom they are to marry.

NOTES

SHAPE OF BOEOTIA, p. 69. Boeotia is the myth-laden province of Thebes where Oedipus unriddled the enigma of the Sphinx and unknowingly married his mother.

THE MAD POMEGRANATE TREE, p. 71
à perdre haleine: "out of breath."

SUN THE FIRST

SAILOR BOY OF THE GARDEN, p. 79
Our Lady of the Annunciation: See note to "The Lord Will Provide" in "Age of Blue Memory," above.
Bouboulína: Heroine of the Greek War of Independence, from the island of Spétsas.

HALF-SUNKEN BOATS, p. 80
Virgin Mary . . . fiesta: August 15, the Dormition of the Virgin, marks the end of a fifteen-day fast in her honor. Pilgrimages are made to the two great shrines of Greek Orthodoxy, to the Church of a Hundred Gates on the Aegean island of Páros, and to the miracle-working icon of the Virgin in her church on the Aegean island of Tínos.

THE ORANGE GIRL, p. 82. Part IV of "Variations on a Sunbeam" in seven parts.

HEROIC AND ELEGIAC SONG, p. 87
VI. Spat on him: In the Greek baptismal ceremony, according to medieval belief and practice, the infant is spat on thrice to indicate the eviction of the devil through the mouth.
VII. Akrokerávnia: Mountains in Albania.
X. Androútsos: Odysseus Androútsos, one of the greatest and most violent guerrilla fighters of the Greek War of Independence.
XI. feathers . . . foreheads: The Italian fascist soldiers wore the feather of a black crow on their hats or helmets.
Or a mother's . . . of Death: Hemmed in by the Turks during the Greek War of Independence, the women of the Zállongo Mountains in Soúli danced their ring dance at the edge of a precipice. At each turn of the dance, a woman with her infant in her arms would hurl herself down the precipice to her death rather than fall into the hands of the Turks. A stone monument of the dancing women, by the sculptor George Zongolópoulos, in abstract style, has been erected on the edge of the cliff.

AXION ESTI

GENESIS III, p. 101
Íos . . . Mílos: Cycladic islands.

GENESIS IV, p. 102
Virgin's colt: The praying mantis.

chick-pea: This plant has been chosen arbitrarily, for neither Elýtis nor anyone else seems to know to what plant the Greek word refers!

GENESIS V, p. 103

Roes . . . Yeltis: Anagrams for Eros, Sea, Marína, Immortality, Elýtis.

PSALM II, p. 106. The Greek language is referred to from Homer, through the Byzantine period, to modern Greece.

Hymn: "Hymn to Liberty" by Dionýsios Solomós, 1798–1857, from the opening quatrain of which the Greek National Hymn has been composed. The opening verses are: "I know you by the cutting edge / Of your dread sword, / I know you by the visage / That strides the earth with violence. / Drawn out of the sacred / Bones of the Greeks, / And as valorous as at first, / Hail, hail O Liberty!"

cracking of eggs: The red Easter "eggs of Resurrection," as they are called, are believed to have miraculous qualities. In some places in Greece, they are placed at Easter beneath the tabernacle that represents the tomb of Christ, so that the joyful "Christ is risen" can be uttered over them. It is a common Easter custom for one to tap the end of his egg against that held by another person. Whoever succeeds in cracking someone else's egg wins and may claim it as his own.

ODES, pp. 107, 108, 109. The stanzas of each ode are not composed of lines containing a set number of metrical accents, but of lines identical in syllable count only, exactly parallel and repeated from stanza to stanza, as in many hymns of the Byzantine period. Furthermore, on either side of an ornament that divides each line, the number of syllables often varies but is repeated with exactitude in each stanza. That is, in a single line there may be three syllables in the first half-line before the ornament, and seven in the half-line following the ornament. This pattern is then repeated exactly in other, parallel stanzas. No two odes are alike, and each introduces some new form of variation. The stresses at the end of each half-line are repeated from stanza to stanza, whether iambic ($\smile$ $-$) or trochaic ($-$ $\smile$) or dactylic ($-$ $\smile$ $\smile$). For instance, Ode 5 in the original Greek is composed of six triplets; each half-line of each triplet has seven syllables, and each half-line ends with a trochee. Ode 7 is composed of three stanzas, the first and last of which have identical patterns of six lines each, and in which the half-lines end with varied accents arranged in a repeated pattern; the last two lines are variations of a refrain. The middle stanza, since it is not repeated, repeats itself by having

NOTES

a similar number of syllables in the half-lines on either side of the ornament; in addition, the accents at the end of each half-line of the first three lines are dissimilarly placed, but similarly placed in each half-line of the other six lines. Ode 11 is composed of four stanzas which are all identical in patterns of both syllable count and accentual endings. Some words in this ode are separated syllabically in relevant places by the ornament. In my translations of these odes I have kept to a syllable count and pattern, though not that of the originals, but have not kept the terminal accentual patterns.

ODE 7, p. 108

Haggith's son: Adonijah, David's son by Haggith, who tried to usurp the throne while David was dying, but the king named his younger son, Solomon, the heir. See 2 Sam., chap. 1.

ODE 11, p. 109

Bucephalos: A giant horse tamed by Alexander the Great in his youth, which became his famous and beloved horse in war.

PROPHETIC, p. 110

Síkinos: A Cycladic island in the Aegean Sea.

Arete: See Introduction, p. 23.

PSALM XVII, p. 112

hosannahs for my coming: See John 12:12–13. "On the next day much people that were come to the feast, when they heard that Jesus was coming to Jerusalem, took branches of palm trees, and went forth to meet him and cried Hosannah: Blessed is the King of Israel that cometh in the name of the Lord."

PSALM XVIII, p. 113

holy, holy: See John, Rev. 4:8. "Holy, holy, holy, Lord God Almighty, which was, and is, and is to come."

Prince of Lilies: Reference to a Minoan mural at Knossos of a young man walking amid lilies.

Laws: Oblique reference to Plato's *Laws.*

Now and Aye: From the most common refrain in the liturgy of the Greek Orthodox Church: "Glory to the Father, and to the Son, and to the Holy Spirit, now and aye, and to the Ages of Ages, Amen."

Worthy it is: See Introduction, p. 25.

GLORIA, p. 114. The quatrains contain uneven syllable counts, but four beats to a line whether we measure by metrical accents or rhetorical stresses. All have feminine endings, except the quatrain before the last in each section, which has a dactylic ending. The lines are primarily iambic-anapestic, with the addition of weak syllables here and there. The couplets, but for a few exceptions, differ in the number of rhetorical stresses from section to section; in addition, each couplet of the first section begins with a "Hail," of the second section with a "He" (the Poet), and of the third section with an "Aye." In the triplets, each line contains three rhetorical stresses and names three things (with the single exception of one line, which has only two stresses): sea, winds, islands, flowers, girls, ships, mountains, and trees. I have translated here all but the first six quatrains and the first triplet of the first section, keeping to an analogous structure.

Slender Girl in Hades: In the demotic song known by this title, the Slender Girl (Λυγερή) begs three gallant lads who are planning to break out of Hades to take her with them, for her parents and relatives must be grieving for her. But they tell her that both parents and relatives have forgotten her, occupied with their mundane affairs or with enjoyments.

Black Number: Which amounts to nothingness, or to evil.

Korai: See note to "Kore of Euthydikos" in "Origin of Landscape," below.

Now, aye: See note to "Psalm XVIII," above.

SIX AND ONE REMORSES FOR THE SKY

SLEEP OF THE VALIANT (Variation), p. 122

Arete: See Introduction, p. 23.

ORIGIN OF LANDSCAPE, p. 124

Kore of Euthydikos: One of the twenty or so statues of archaic maidens found on the Akropolis. This one, nicknamed "The Little Pouting Girl," is from the early fifth century.

SEVEN DAYS FOR ETERNITY, p. 126

Calf Bearer: Statue from the Akropolis, ca. 575–550 B.C., of a young man holding a calf by its legs, draped around his shoulders.

Stalk of Wheat: Demeter, the fertility goddess, gave Triptolomos the first grain of wheat, taught him the arts of harnessing oxen to the plough, of sowing the soil with grain, and of making bread. He is depicted in many bas reliefs and vase paintings holding aloft an ear of grain.

Battle of the 1 and the 9: That is, between the two extremities of a decade.

VILLA NATACHA, p. 131. See Introduction, p. 31. "Tériade" is a French contraction of the surname of Efstrátis Eleftheriádhis, born in Mitilíni, the ancient Lesbos, where on his estate he has built a museum to house his various publications. The gardens surrounding his Villa Natacha have become so renowned that he is known as "The Man of Gardens."

seas also communicate from afar: Joining the two regions of the Mediterranean, that around Tériade's estate in Mitilíni and the one on Cap-Ferret.

Do not forget me . . . Anaktoría: Sappho of Lesbos addresses one of her poems to her beautiful and faithless friend, Anaktoría, who left her in order to marry a soldier and follow him to Sardis, in Lydia. In the poem she begs Anaktoría not to forget her.

water . . . Saint Paraskeví: In the church of Saint Paraskeví on Tériade's estate in Mitilíni, a well bubbles up in one of its corners.

Theófilos: "Theófilos Hadzimihaíl (1868–1934), the foremost Greek Primitive painter, was born in Mitilíni where he painted murals in many homes and taverns. He was befriended and helped by Tériade, who has now built a museum for the painter's work on his estate and given it to the town of Mitilíni.

Èze and Cap-Estel: From a terrace of the Villa Natacha, the regions of Èze and Cap-Estel can be seen extending toward Monte Carlo.

Prince: Tériade.

DEATH AND RESURRECTION OF CONSTANDINOS PALEO-LOGHOS, p. 137. See Introduction, p. 32.

THE LIGHT TREE

PALM SUNDAY, p. 141. See note to "hosannahs for my coming" in "Psalm XVII," above.

DELOS, p. 142. See Introduction, p. 34.

THREE TIMES THE TRUTH, p. 143

Nobody: In Book IX of Homer's *Odyssey*, lines 364–67, Polyphemos, the Cyclops, asks Odysseus for his name, and he replies: "My name is Nobody. That is what I am called by my mother and father and by all my friends." Elýtis uses the ancient word Οὖτις instead of the modern Greek word Κανείς.

THE ODYSSEY, p. 147.

the purple waves . . . ship sped on: At the end of Book II of *The Odyssey*, lines 427–28, Athena sends a steady wind to help Telemachus on his way to find his father.

Thales of Miletos: Greek sage and philosopher, fl. seventh and sixth centuries B.C. The historical Seven Wise Men began with Thales.

Ibn Al-Mansour: Arabian Caliph, founder of Bagdad (712?–775).

Simeon the young Theologian: See *The Penguin Book of Greek Verse*, edited by Constantine Trypanis (Penguin Books, 1971),

Introduction, p. liv: "Of all the post-iconoclast religious poets, Symeon the Mystic (949–1022) ranks highest. After Romanos he is the second figure of importance in Byzantine poetry, because of his striking originality. His long mystical hymns are inspired and sincere pieces of writing, in spite of a cumbersome formlessness and many tedious repetitions. Symeon is also a milestone in the history of Greek metre, for he is the first to use in personal poetry the 'political' fifteen-syllable line, the verse which was to become supreme, almost exclusive, in later Greek demotic poetry. The origins of this verse are obscure, but it appears to go back to the early days of the Eastern Empire, or even further."

Paracelsus: His real name was Theophrastus Bombastus von Hohenheim, Swiss chemist and physician (1493–1541).

Hardenberg: Hardenberg von Friedrich, German author (1772–1801) who wrote under the pseudonym of Novalis.

George the Fisherman: Representative of the Greek peasant.

André Breton: 1896–1966, founder of surrealism.

The Rose of Espahan and famous Pharizad: Two heroines of *A Thousand and One Nights.*

vienlaviéla: Exact transliteration from the Greek. A seed plant, also in fossilized form, named after the botanist Wieland.

Osman: Founder of the Ottoman Empire (1259–1326).

Nikephóros Phocás: Byzantine emperor of the tenth century.

triclínium: The throne room, although Elýtis uses the word for the throne itself. The poet is comparing plants and flowers to sabres and thrones.

peacock: Byzantine emperors had such artificial and mechanical birds. See Yeats' "Sailing to Byzantium."

CYCLICAL, p. 153.

Mount Tabor: The mountain in Palestine where the transfiguration of Christ took place.

THE GARDEN OF THE SCORCHED HAND, p. 153.

iaí iatataí: Cries of grief in ancient Greek tragedy.

Phison, Gihon, Tigris, Euphrates: The four rivers of Paradise.

THE SOVEREIGN SUN, p. 167. The nursery rhyme from which Elýtis took the opening and meter for *The Sovereign Sun* begins thus:

Ο ἥλιος ὅ ἡλιάτορας

Ο πετροπαιχνιδιάτορας

ἡλιάτορας and πετροπαιχνιδιάτορας are words such as children invent and play with. The first is a combination of the word for sun, ἥλιος, and a suffix, -άτορας, as in ἀντοκράτορας, meaning em-

peror. The second word is a combination of stone-play-átoras. A
literal translation of the nursery rhyme would be:

> The sun, the emperor sun
> the champion stone player
> holds a knife and a sword
> and goes to Pétros' courtyard
> and says: "O María, O Sophía,
> where are Pétros' children?"
> "I washed and combed their hair
> then sent them off to school."
> "What have you done with their shorn hair?"
> "I hung it on an olive tree."
> ' And where is this olive tree?"
> "Fire burnt it down."
> "And where is this fire?"
> "Water put it out."
> "And where is that water?"
> "The calf drank it up."
> "And where is that calf?"
> "Down by Saint Nicholas
> Where it keeps company
> with a red fez.
> It has a pig that grunts,
> it has a hen that cackles,
> it has a rooster that crows,
> and María pees in her panties."

BIBLIOGRAPHY

BIBLIOGRAPHY

A complete list of books, periodicals, newspapers, and interviews by or about Elýtis in Greek, and all that has been translated of his works or written about him in other languages can be found in Mario Vitti's *A Bibliography of Odysseus Elýtis* (Athens: Íkaros, forthcoming). The brief bibliography that follows contains only the most essential material, primarily in books and anthologies; only some articles in English and American periodicals, at times accompanied by translations of the poetry, have been noted. The arrangement is chronological.

IN GREEK
I. Poems by Elýtis in Book Form, Broadsheet, and Periodicals

Προσανατολισμοὶ [Orientations]. Athens: Pirsós, December 1939, 180 pp. Athens: Galaxy Editions, June 1961, 130 pp.

Ἥλιος ὁ πρῶτος, μαζὶ μὲ τὶς παραλλαγὲς πάνο σὲ μιὰν ἀχτίδα [*Sun the First together with Variations on a Sunbeam*]. Athens: The Gull, December 1943, 44 pp.

"Ἆσμα ἡρωικὸ καὶ πένθιμο γιὰ τὸν χαμένο ἀνθυπολοχαγὸ τῆς 'Αλβανίας" ["Heroic and Elegiac Song for the Lost Second Lieutenant of the Albanian Campaign"] In *Notebook*, no. 2, Athens, August–September 1945, pp. 9–13. Athens: Íkaros, December 1962, 40 pp.

"Ἡ καλωσύνη στὶς λυκοπορίες" ["Kindness in the Wolfpasses"]. In *Notebook*, Athens, December 1946, pp. 3–14.

Ἄξιον ἐστὶ [*Áxion Estí*]. Athens: Íkaros, December 1959, 94 pp.

Ἔξη καὶ μιὰ τύψεις γιὰ τὸν οὐρανὸ [*Six and One Remorses for the Sky*]. Athens: Íkaros, February 1960, 30 pp.

"'Αλβανιάδα. Ποίημα γιὰ δύο φωνές. Μέρος πρῶτο" ["Albanian. Poems for Two Voices. First Part"]. In Πανσπουδαστικὴ, no. 41, December 25, 1962, pp. 11–14.

"Θάνατος καὶ 'Ανάστασις τοῦ Κωνσταντίνου Παλαιολόγου" ["Death and Resurrection of Constandínos Paleológhos"]. In *Tram*, Thessa-

191

loníki, December 1971, pp. 30–32. Geneva: Duo d'Art S. A., December 1971. 16 pp. Silk-screen handwritten text and four embossed designs by Cóstas Colentianós, Chavannes-sur-Reyssouze. One hundred eleven copies on paper velin d'arches, numbered and signed by the artist and the poet. Copies 1–11 not for sale.

Τὸ Μονόγραμμα [The Monogram]. Famagústa, Cyprus: L'Oiseau, 1971. 32 pp. Printed in the poet's handwriting by Joseph Adam, Brussels. Athens: Íkaros, December 1972, 32 pp.

Ὁ ἥλιος ὁ ἡλιάτορας [The Sovereign Sun]. Athens: Íkaros, December 1971, 32 pp.

Τὸ φωτόδεντρο καὶ ἡ δέκατη τέταρτη ὀμορφιὰ [The Light Tree and the Fourteenth Beauty]. Athens: Íkaros, December 1971, 70 pp.

Τὰ ρῶ τοῦ ἔρωτα [The Ro of Eros]. Athens: Asterías, November 1972, 98 pp.

Villa Natacha. Thessaloníki: Tram, June 1973, 20 pp. With an original sketch by Picasso, a colored lithograph by Laurens, and decorations by Matisse from the periodical Verve.

Ὁ φυλλομάντης [The Leaf Diviner]. Broadsheet. Athens: Asterías, December 1973.

II. Prose Works by Elýtis in Book Form
Ὁ ζωγράφος Θεόφιλος [The Painter Theófilos]. Athens: Asterías, December 1973.

Ἀνοιχτὰ φύλλα [Open Book]. Athens: Asterías, 1974, 450 pp.

III. Books about Elýtis
Lilí Zoghráfou. The Sundrinker Elýtis. Athens: Ermías, May 1971, 96 pp.

Tásos Lighnádhis. Elýtis' Áxion Estí: Introduction, Commentary, Analysis. Psihikón, Athens: Library of the Moraítis School, Spring–Summer 1971, 308 pp. With a diagram of the poem's structure and sixteen photographs illustrating some images and references in the text.

Yórghos Thalásis. The Perfumer's Art. Athens: Estía, 1974, 72 pp.

IV. Commentary in Book Form
Kléon Paráskhos. Greek Lyric Poets. Athens: 1953.

S. Spandhonídhis. The Newer Poetry in Greece. Athens: Íkaros, 1955.

Andréas Karandónis. Introduction to the Newer Poetry. Athens: Dhífros, 1958. Athens: Galaxy Editions, 1971.

Andréas Karandónis. Round about Contemporary Greek Poetry. Athens, 1961.

BIBLIOGRAPHY

M. G. Meraklís. *Loneliness and Poetry: Greek Lyrical Speech in the Last Two Decades.* Athens, 1961.
Yánnis Kordhátos. *History of Neo-Hellenic Literature, 1453–1961.* 2 vols. Athens, 1962.
Yórghos Thémelis. *Our Newer Poetry.* Athens: Féxis, 1963.
Pános Thasítis. *Round about Poetry.* Thessaloníki, 1966.
Ilías Petrópoulos. *Elýtis, Móralis, Tsaroúhis.* Thessaloníki, 1966.
M. G. Meraklís. *Contemporary Greek Literature, 1945–1970,* vol. 1. Thessaloníki, 1971.
Loúla Kotsétsou. *Portraits of Our Literature,* vol. 2. Athens, 1971.
Pávlos Nikodhímos. *Concise Review of Neo-Hellenic Literature.* Athens: Nikodhímos, 1972.
Níkos Pappás. *The True History of Neo-Hellenic Literature, 1100–1973.* Athens: Tíflis, 1974.

IN ENGLISH

I. Translations and Commentary in Book Form
New World Writing No. 2. Translations by Kimon Friar. New York: New American Library, November 1952.
Little Treasure of World Poetry. Edited by Hugh Creekmore. Translations by Kimon Friar. New York: Scribner's, 1952.
Six Poets of Modern Greece. Translations and Introduction by Edmund Keeley and Philip Sherrard. London: Thames & Hudson, 1960. New York: Knopf, 1961.
The Pursuit of Greece. By Philip Sherrard. London, 1964.
Four Greek Poets. Translations by Edmund Keeley and Philip Sherrard. Harmondsworth, Middlesex, England: Penguin Books, 1966. Same selections from Elýtis as in *Six Poets of Modern Greece.*
Modern European Poetry. General editor, Willis Barnstone. Greek section translated by Kimon Friar. New York: Bantam Books, 1966.
Modern Greece. By John Campbell and Philip Sherrard. London, 1968.
Introduction to Modern Greek Literature. General editor, Mary Gianos. Poetry selection translated by Kimon Friar. New York: Twayne Publishers, 1969.
Modern Greek Poetry. Translations by Rae Dalven. 2d ed. revised and enlarged. New York: Russell & Russell, 1971. Inaccurate translations.
The Penguin Book of Greek Verse. Bilingual, with prose translations. Introduced and edited by Constantine A. Trypanis. Harmondsworth, Middlesex, England: Penguin Books, 1971.

II. Translations and Commentary in Periodicals

Horizon. London, March 1946. "Modern Greek Poetry" by Nános Valaorítis.

The Listener. London, August 16, 1951. "The Unresolved Past" by Kay Cicellis.

Wake 12. Boston, Winter 1953. "The Greek Tradition" and translations by Kimon Friar.

Accent. Urbana, Ill., Summer 1954. "Odysseus Elýtis" and translations by Kimon Friar; two letters by Odysseus Elýtis.

The Charioteer. New York, Autumn 1960. Translations by Kimon Friar, and "Odysseus Elytis: A Critical Mosaic" by Mítsos Papanikoláou, Andréas Karandónis, Samuel Baud-Bovy, Nános Valaorítis, Kimon Friar, and Níkos Gátsos.

Poetry. Chicago, October 1964. " 'The Genesis': A Commentary" by Edmund Keeley, and translations by Edmund Keeley, Philip Sherrard, and Ruth Whitman.

Books Abroad. Spring 1971. "Odysseus Elýtis" and translations by Kimon Friar. With a photograph by Lütfi Öskök.

Books Abroad. Summer 1973. Book reviews by Kimon Friar of *The Light Tree and the Fourteenth Beauty, Death and Resurrection of Constandínos Paleológhos,* and of Tásos Lighnádhis' *Elýtis' Áxion Estí.*

Books Abroad. Autumn 1973. Book review by Kimon Friar of *The Monogram.*

Books Abroad. Winter 1973. Book review by Kimon Friar of *The Ro of Eros* and *The Sovereign Sun.*

III. Dissertations

The "Áxion Estí" of Odysseus Elýtis. Translated and annotated with an introduction by George Niketas. University of Georgia, Athens, Georgia, 1967.

IN FOREIGN LANGUAGES

I. Translations in Book Form

Pòemes. Bilingual. Translations by Robert Levesque. Athens: Estía, February 1945.

Poesie precedute del canto eroico e funebre per il sottotenente caduta in Albania. Translated by Mario Vitti. Rome: Il Presente, June 1952.

Körper des Sommers. Selected poems translated by Antigone Kasoléa and Barbara Schlörb. St. Gallen, Switzerland: Tschudy-Verlag, 1960.

Elitis, 21 Poesie. Translations by Vincenzo Rotolo. Palermo: Istituto Siciliano di Studi Bizantini e Neoellenici, June 1968.

To Áxion Estí—Gepriesen Sei. Translated by Günter Dietz. Hamburg Düsseldorf: Claassen Verlag, 1969.

II. Translations and Commentary in Book Form

Domaine Grec (1930–1946). By Robert Levesque. Geneva and Paris: Éditions des Trois Collines, 1947.

Anthologie de poètes néogrecs. By Marie-Louise Arserin. Rome, 1959.

Griechische Lyric der Gegenwart. By Otto Stainingir. Linz: J. Wimmer, 1960.

Grecia 60. Poesia a verdad. By Jaime García Terrés. Alacená, Mexico, 1962.

Poesia greca del '900. By Mario Vitti. Parma: Ugo Guanda Editore, 1957. Revised, 1966.

La litteratura griega medieval y moderna. By José Alsino and Carlo Miralles. Barcelona, 1966.

Storia della letteratura neogreca. By Mario Vitti. Turin: ERI, 1971.

Antologia de la literatura neohelenica. I. Poesia. By Miguel Castillo Didier. Santiago, Chile, 1971.

ACKNOWLEDGMENTS

ACKNOWLEDGMENTS

I am deeply obligated to the poet for his assistance in the translation of these poems. When I first arrived in Greece in 1946, he was among the first poets I met and began translating. During the past twenty-seven years we have met frequently in various confectionary shops and taverns around Constitution Square in Athens, in the coffee room of the King George Hotel, in his apartment in Athens, and finally on the island of Aegina, working on the poems at his hotel or on small iron tables of sweet shops by the sea promenade. My practice was to translate a poem literally, at the same time composing lists of synonyms and adding questions along the margins of my translations or his books, and then to meet with him to discuss various possibilities and work out subtleties of meaning. When I was in the United States and he in Greece, I would send him lists of questions and he would answer by return mail. After I had completed what I considered my final draft, we would examine the poems again, and after the lapse of months and years, once again. I am grateful to Odysseus Elýtis because, although he has gently complained about my delays, he has never made me feel impelled to publish my translations before I have felt satisfied with them. What understanding I may have of his poems is due, not only to the close reading which translation imposes, but also to the letters he has written me about his work and to our discussions about his intentions, methods, technique.

I should also like to thank his friend and fellow poet Níkos Gátsos, who, when Elýtis was not available, would go over many of the poems with me, giving me always his honest and meticulous advice. Others who have helped me immeasurably are Andónis Decaválles and Násos Vayanás. I am also indebted to other translators of Elýtis, in particular Edmund Keeley and Philip Sherrard. Acknowledgment is due to the following periodicals where some of these translations have appeared: *Accent, Atlantic Monthly, Boundary 2, Fulbright Review, Kyak, The Charioteer, Greek Heritage, Mundus Artium, Poetry* (Chicago), *Quarterly Review of Literature,* and *Wake;* and to the following anthologies: *New World Writing No. 2* (New World Library, 1952); *Little Treasury of World Poetry,* edited by Hugh Creekmore (Scribner's, 1962); *Modern European Poetry,* edited by Willis Barnstone (Bantam Books, 1966); *Introduction to Modern Greek Literature,* edited by Mary Gianos (Twayne, 1969); and *Modern Greek Poetry,* translated by Kimon Friar (Simon & Schuster, 1973).